Play Great Rock Guitar

Jam, Shred, and Riff in 10 Foolproof Lessons

Phil Capone
Paul Copperwaite

Billboard Books/New York

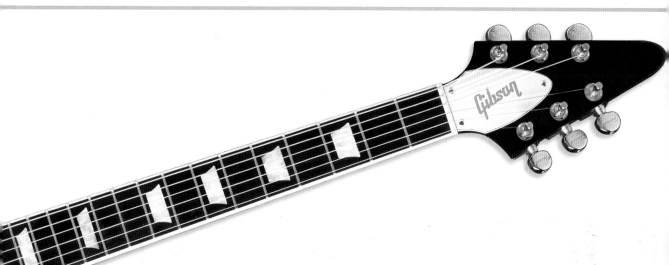

Play Great Rock Guitar

First edition for North America published in 2010 by
Billboard Books

Published in the United States by Billboard Books, an
imprint of the Crown Publishing Group, a division of
Random House, Inc., New York.
www.crownpublishing.com

BILLBOARD is a registered trademark of Nielsen Business
Media, Inc.

Library of Congress Control Number: 2010929179
ISBN: 978-0-8174-0007-1

Conceived, designed, and produced by
Marshall Editions
The Old Brewery
6 Blundell Street
London N7 9BH
www.marshalleditions.com

All original songs composed by
Paul Copperwaite and Dan Lack
Additional guitar playing by Dan Lack
Audio recording by John Hall and George Stuart

Commissioning Editor: Laura Price
Art Director: Ivo Marloh
Design: The Urban Ant Ltd.
Picture Manager: Veneta Bullen
Production: Nikki Ingram

Color separation by Modern Age
Repro House Ltd., Hong Kong
Printed in China by 1010
Printing International Ltd.

10 9 8 7 6 5 4 3 2 1

To Daisy, my relative minor, with love from Paul

Contents

Getting Started

The following chapter aims to equip you with the knowledge you need to spend your budget wisely. Maybe you've received a guitar as a gift and are wondering what other gear will help you get the best out of it. Otherwise, you're looking to make a crucial purchase—your first electric guitar! Enjoy the buying experience—it's your opportunity to check out the vast range of styles, shapes, and tones that the market affords. So savor it—there's no need to rush into an impulse buy.

Keep the style of music you want to play in mind. That may sound obvious, but it's easily overlooked in the moment. We're not just talking appearances here; areas of choice to bear in mind include: body type; pickups; your optimal neck shape and fingerboard radius (see page 13); effects and accessories, and what type (see page 18).

Like a good pair of walking shoes, a classic all-arounder such as a Stratocaster or singlecut (Les Paul)–style guitar will suit most purposes and date the least. Go for classic rather than the latest fad (especially when it comes to seven- and eight-string guitars), at least at first. Select by build quality rather than faddish features and your first guitar really could last you a lifetime, however many others you acquire as time goes by.

B.C. Rich Warlock

The B.C. Rich Warlock's distinct shape makes it immediately recognizable. Slayer's Kerry King is a fan, so much so that B.C. Rich now makes a Kerry King–design guitar. Other notable players include Mick Thomson of Slipknot and Paul Stanley of Kiss. This is obviously a new guitar—note the plastic covers on the pickups.

How To
Use This Book

This book has been designed to enable you to learn guitar simply, painlessly, and at your own pace. You will discover the secrets of the electric guitarist, how to write your own killer riffs, play soaring lead lines, and even compose your own songs.

As you work your way through the chapters, you'll see that every exercise has a sound file to go along with it, which you'll find on the accompanying CD. Many text-only exercises can leave you wondering if your playing sounds exactly right, even when it does. With this book you can proceed with the next exercise, confident that you got the last one right!

Rules are your friends. Learn them first—you can always break them later. They are just quick ways of summing up centuries of humankind's knowledge and experience of music. A lot of guitarists starting out voice the worry that learning will somehow inhibit their inspiration and feel for the music. While it's true that the great bluesmen often are not able to tell you the names of the notes from which they wring so much feeling, this doesn't mean that, even if you do fill your head with theory, you can't choose to ignore it and take the "feel" approach when you want to. Learning does not kill passion—it lets you express your passion better.

When all is said and done, your ears are the final judge. If it comes down to a choice between what a book like this says is right and what sounds good to you, then go with the latter—this *is* rock 'n' roll.

Chords
Chord shapes are illustrated by dots on a fretboard. Red dots indicate tonic notes. Numbers within the dots refer to the fingers on your fretting hand (1, your index finger, through 4, your little finger). Numbers below the fretboard indicate frets.

Boxes
Boxed text throughout highlights extra information, rock star and band info, and essential asides.

Scales
Scales are shown as dots on a fretboard with occasional fingering supplied where necessary.

Notes
Tonic notes are shown in red, others in yellow.

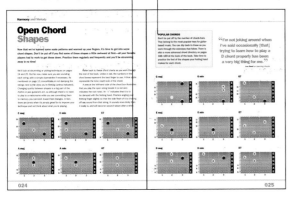

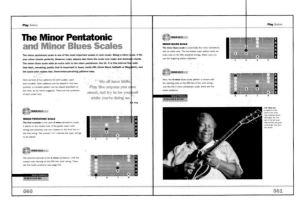

A NOTE ON HANDEDNESS

There are exceptions to the convention of using the terms "strumming" or "picking hand" and "fretting hand" throughout this book, since there are times when you aren't doing these respective actions. To avoid confusion, we will speak in the lessons as if to the right-handed guitarist.

Dick Dale

Dubbed the "King of the Surf Guitar," Dale was a left-handed player initially forced to play a right-handed model, much like Jimi Hendrix. However, Dale did so without re-stringing the guitar, which meant he effectively played it upside down. Even after he acquired a left-handed guitar, Dale continued to use reverse stringing.

THE NASHVILLE NUMBERING SYSTEM

In discussion of tab and musical composition, Arabic numerals—1, 2, 3, etc.—indicate the note of the scale; Roman numerals—I, IV, V—indicate the chords built on each note. A chord indicated under this system has the tonality (major or minor) derived from its position within the scale, so a II chord will always be minor, or a VII chord diminished, for example.

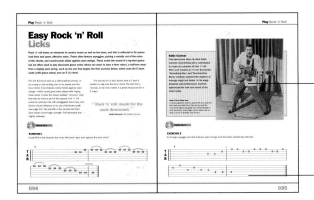

Heroes
Each style of playing highlights the icons of the genre with notes on their playing style and musical impact.

Exercises
Each exercise comes with tab notation to help you play at a glance.

Choosing
Your Guitar

Learning a musical instrument is a challenge; there's no need to make it any harder by learning on a poor-quality instrument. Even Kirk Hammett would have thrown in the towel if he'd spent his early days battling with some unplayable old axe! So let our suggestions guide you into making exactly the right purchase—we promise you won't regret it.

There's an incredible range of electric guitars on the market today. And, thanks to the high standard of most of the Far Eastern manufacturers, you don't have to pay an arm and a leg to get a good one. There are also plenty of second-hand bargains to be had. However, you should be wary of buying your axe online unless it's from a local seller who will allow you to "try before you buy." We think

of acoustic guitars as being as fragile and delicate as the folkies who play them, but electric guitars aren't exactly bulletproof. So it's crucial to make sure that a used instrument has been well kept and isn't being sold because it's a "lemon." The most important thing to remember is that you'll need an instrument that is comfortable to play (weird shapes may look cool, but have

Fender
Telecaster

Fender
Stratocaster

Gretsch
Nashville

Rickenbacker
325C58JG

Gibson Flying V

you ever tried sitting down to practice with a Flying-V?) and is capable of creating a wide range of sounds. A good guitar will make you want to play it; it will also grow with you as your musical tastes inevitably broaden. Some helpful pointers as to types of guitar follow—you can think of them almost like a tree diagram. But first, some observations that apply to all guitars:

Find one with an even temper. Intonation is the degree to which your guitar is in tune with itself. Poor intonation may mean that the guitar is in need of a good setup, or has a problem that can't be solved, invariably with the neck. Guitars like this are best avoided altogether, unless an experienced guitar player whom you trust is sure it's fixable. Poor intonation means that although chords played in open positions may sound in tune, intervals (i.e., anything more than a single note) that you play in higher fret positions will be out of tune within themselves, and even single notes will sound out of tune with other musicians (leading those who aren't aware of intonation issues to keep tuning and retuning their instruments). Jokes about Pete Townshend–style guitar-smashing sessions aside, instruments in tune with themselves are described as being "well tempered." A guide to checking intonation is given on page 16, but it's vital to mention its importance at the buying stage.

Make good salespeople work for you. Unlike a stereo or a refrigerator, a guitar straight out of the box is not always ready to use. Even reputable manufacturers work on the basis that each buyer will want to set up their own guitar. Although you will learn how to tinker with your guitars as time goes by, set some time and money aside at this stage for the guitar store to give your new instrument some TLC—or why not negotiate the setup as part of the deal with the store?

Guitar stores are your friends: a good salesperson will be used to people who are starting out, so don't think you have to put up with a competitive, superior attitude. If it helps, ask him or her to play the guitar for you (preferably something close to your own tastes rather than their own killer licks, and at low gain), though be aware they may put it through the best valve amp in the store! Ideally, take a guitar-playing buddy with you.

Good intonation will mean your guitar has a straight neck. Check the newness of the frets on secondhand instruments: grooved frets beneath each string can mean fret-buzz, and a re-fret can be costly.

Try before you buy. The Internet offers many great-looking deals, but each guitar is different, and its style offers no clue as to how it actually plays. Plus, you are consigning your new purchase to being shipped, which is no problem for a robust effects pedal but perilous for your new axe. Besides, out there in cyberspace, things are not always what they seem. So if you must buy online, do so from reputable Internet retailers, and be aware of how easy it is for the unscrupulous to build a great-looking fake and sell it on popular auction sites. Some of these are fun guitars in their own right—but a huge disappointment if they are not what you thought you were buying. Passing them off as originals is a criminal offense, too.

Guitar Anatomy

Since this book is about rock guitar, we'll gloss over the wonderful world of acoustics, even though, as we'll see, many playing styles—such as drop-D tuning, for example—are highly useful for the heaviest metal as well as the most dyed-in-the-wool folk music. At this stage, you face two areas of choice: the tones you aim to have at your fingertips, and the guitar's physical features that best assist your playing comfort and speed.

Pickups: Possibly the biggest single influence on tone (aside from your playing) is your choice of pickup. Broadly, these consist of bar magnets (with or without pole pieces for each string) wound with wire, and your guitar's steel strings vibrate within their magnetic field. Classic guitars traditionally equipped with these single-coil pickups include the Fender Stratocaster and Telecaster. The second broad group features double-coil pickups, which consist of two magnets placed next to each other. These feature on rock staples the Gibson Les Paul and SG guitars, among many others. Originally invented to minimize the slight ungrounded hum—more of a buzz, really—that single coils produce when you remove your hands from the strings, they're more commonly known as "humbuckers," and were increasingly bought for their tone rather than this now-incidental feature. There are other pickup types, such as P90s (along with variations such as active electronics and MIDI or piezo pickups), but electric pickup choices are best explained in terms of these two.

Single-coil: generally twangy, thinner-sounding, with more audible pick/finger sounds, and cuts through a band's mix with great effect. Clean: think Dick Dales's twangy surf guitar style or Nile Rodgers's infectious funk rhythm work. Overdriven: think Jimi Hendrix's awesome soloing style or Stevie Ray Vaughan's fiery blues licks.

Humbucker: darker, thicker-sounding, more "smokey," often with more sustain and a little more resonance in the attack. Chugs along beautifully but can get muddy in a mix. Clean: think Pat Metheny's fat jazz tone or B.B. King's inimitable blues licks. Overdriven: think Eric Clapton's "woman tone" with Cream or Tony Iommi's deep, drop-tuned riffs with Black Sabbath.

Bodies and necks: The woods used—commonly alder, ash, basswood, maple, or mahogany—have a great tonal influence too, although a classy Les Paul with lousy pickups will have a weaker sound when amplified than a plywood guitar with great pickups, so once you're playing with a band, an after-market pickup upgrade can be a great, cost-effective way to get some top tones into your arsenal.

Strats, Teles, Les Pauls, and their ilk are solid-body guitars, made from one, two, or three pieces of wood joined together. Semi-solid, semi-acoustic, or thinline guitars—such as Gibson's 335 and 355 models, Epiphone's Casino, or Hofner's President—have hollow bodies. Though used in the blues to great effect by the likes of King and Clapton, they were designed in the jazz age and are prone to feedback at modern stage volumes.

A through-neck design is one in which the sides have been attached to form the body, as opposed to a bolt-on, which allows for a neck-change during the guitar's life, either for preference or in case of warping. Through necks are said to have better sustain, though no single factor clinches the issue that simply.

Neck profiles may be "D"—which is deeper from the fingerboard to the back of the neck than a "C"—while a "V" is self-explanatory. "C" shapes are easier to play than the more clublike "D" (which is said to have more sustain), while a "V" falls between the two in profile.

The larger the radius of the fingerboard (or fretboard), the flatter it is. Smaller radius necks tend to be easier for playing chords and barres (chord shapes that use the flat of the first finger to fret multiple strings) thanks to the way they curve out to meet your fingers, while a flatter fingerboard lends itself better to lead work and string bends. Thicker and taller frets, which are less prone to fret buzz than flatter ones, are also more suited to string bending and will last longer but require more finger strength to play.

Action refers to the distance between the frets and the strings. Higher action is harder to play but gives a more bell-like tone. Knowing this much will give you an idea of what you may prefer, but there's really no substitute for trying out the different types.

String gauges: You're unlikely to encounter anything other than "nines," "tens," or "elevens," where a "ten" is 0.01 of an inch and the number refers to the diameter of the top "E" string in pitch (so, the one nearest your feet). Nines are typically .9, .11, .16, .24, .32, .42, and tens are .10, .13, .17, .26, .36, .46.

The bottom three strings (and sometimes the fourth) are invariably nickel-wound. Lighter strings are easier to play fast, whereas thicker strings give a better tone. (Does that trade-off sound familiar yet?)

Surf maestro Dick Dale, for example, uses very thick strings to maximize the impact of his strong right-hand technique; however, smooth distortion and overdrive tones can make this factor less relevant, allowing for the use of thinner strings to help with your *legato* playing (where notes sustain into each other) such as hammer-ons and pull-offs or tapping techniques.

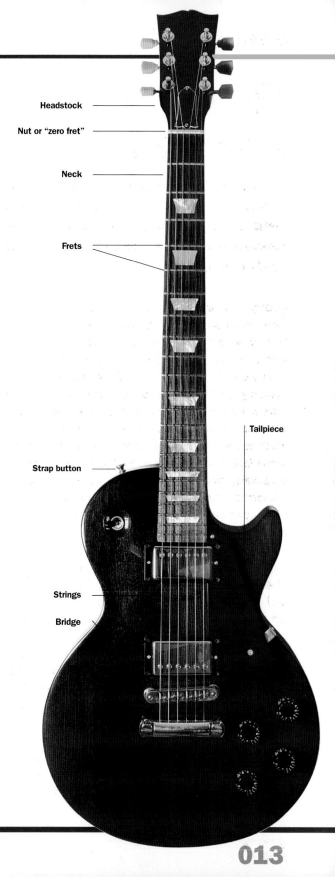

Headstock

Nut or "zero fret"

Neck

Frets

Tailpiece

Strap button

Strings

Bridge

How to Hold
Your Guitar

Whether sitting or standing, comfort and accessibility are your goals. Pretentious though it may sound, how relaxed your muscle fibers are will translate into your playing. Inner calm will lead to greater fluidity in helping you avoid mistakes and really go for those notes with confidence, even if you're playing an aggressive, angry piece. Settle your breathing and think about the piece for a few seconds before you play it. It will help clear your mind of other things. Be warm—cold fingers won't go where you tell them to, while keeping hydrated helps to avoid cramping in your hands and forearms.

Standing
Your guitar should balance well on its shoulder strap without your hands touching it. Having to support the neck to any degree to stop it sliding down is a technique-hampering no-no. Bracing it with the forearm of your picking arm is just as bad.

The higher up your torso you hold your guitar, the easier it is to play, and you will avoid the strain in the wrist of your fretting hand that comes with playing a low-slung axe. If you must do a Johnny Ramone, then angle the neck upward as much as possible.

Sitting
Conventionally, the guitar sits on the same thigh as your strumming hand. A classical guitarist's footstool or small box on which to put this foot can be helpful in preventing your hunching over the guitar but isn't essential. Again, the neck should remain at a good angle without added support. You'll need a little space to one side of you for the body of the guitar to overhang—so you can't use a chair with arms.

Zakk Wylde
Best known as Ozzy Osbourne's guitarist and founder of the heavy metal band Black Label Society, Wylde often plays his guitar with the neck angled high.

Strumming or Picking Hand

Hold your pick between your thumb and forefinger (your hand should be as relaxed as possible without dropping the pick). The most efficient techniques are based on maximizing your economy of movement, which means moving as little as possible relative to the notes you are playing—giving you time to play more! A deeper explanation of techniques can be found on pages 26 and 27.

Slash
The former lead guitarist of the hard rock band Guns N' Roses, Slash's strumming and picking techniques define the sound of many Guns N' Roses songs.

Fretting Hand

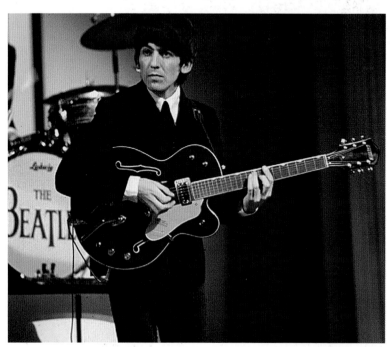

You want your fretting hand to be in a position relative to the guitar neck so that your wrist is in line with the fretboard, not behind it. That way you'll be able to place the very tips of your fingers on any given fret, rather than the pads of your fingertips. Your aim is to be able to fret a string while the strings on either side of it continue to ring. Later we'll look at intentionally damping strings with your fretting-hand fingers.

George Harrison
As lead guitarist for the Beatles, Harrison had a lyrical style of playing that required every note to be clearly sounded.

Tuning

Standard tuning is the most versatile and commonly used tuning for guitar. There are other types, such as open and drop tunings, and we will be examining some of these later in the book. In this lesson you'll learn the best way to get your guitar in standard tuning and ready to play.

TRACK 01

Begin with the low E string (the one nearest your head) and work up to the top E. Try to use your tuning pegs to tune as closely as possible to them. It's great ear training, as are tuning forks and pitch pipes. Today, we're spoiled for choice by electronic tuning devices, from handheld tuners to sophisticated pedal and rack tuners.

For most purposes, especially if a singer is involved, you'll want to play to concert pitch (at which your A string is 440 hertz on the audio spectrum). This is distinct from making sure your guitar is in tune with itself at any pitch, which is known as relative tuning. Relative tuning is a

great way to test whether your guitar is in tune quickly and without the aid of a tuner. Start on the lowest string in pitch (remember, that's the one nearest to your head). Place your finger on the fifth fret and check the pitch with the open A string above; they should sound the same. As before, use the tuning pegs to make any adjustments. The diagram below illustrates how to check each of your strings using relative tuning. Notice how the third string (G) is fretted on the fourth fret, unlike all the other strings. This is because the second and third strings are tuned a major third apart, unlike the other strings, which are a perfect fourth apart.

Intonation

While learning open chords and taking your first steps on the instrument, the limitations of a poorly set up guitar will not be so apparent. But as you begin to play pieces, featuring interesting chord shapes and passages of music played further up the neck and closer to the body of the guitar, intonation factors will come into play. If this happens, don't be put off—it's not your playing!

Checking a guitar's intonation involves listening to make sure that for each string, the harmonic at the 12th fret (which is halfway along the length of each string) is at exactly the same pitch as the open (unfretted) string. If you wonder why the string saddles on your bridge are set at different positions, this is because of the different way each string stretches, going slightly sharp, and it is the saddles that are adjusted to minimize the difference between each fretted note and its harmonic.

Tuning
Invariably, tuning pegs turn counterclockwise to raise the pitch (clockwise for the top three strings of a Gibson-style headstock, as on page 13). Tremolo systems with locking nuts have fine-tuners at the bridge. To tune your guitar, play the bottom E string (the one nearest your head) while fretting the string at the fifth fret. This should sound the same as the unfretted A string. Then play the A string while fretting the string at the fifth fret. This should sound the same as the unfretted D string, and so on for all strings, except the G string, which is fretted at the fourth fret and should sound the same as the unfretted B string.

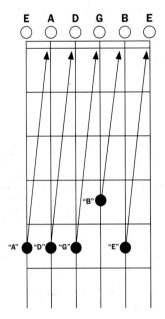

Reading Tab

Chances are, if you've already checked out what's involved in playing the guitar, especially online, you've come across standard tab. It's not capable of encapsulating all musical ideas, like traditional notation, but is a great teaching aid, especially in conjunction with being able to hear a track—and it is purely visual.

Six horizontal lines represent the guitar's strings. The numbers are read left to right and simply represent the frets to be played on each string—it's that simple!

Some CD tracks repeat the tab, others have an extra note to show you how the riff or lick repeats or resolves.

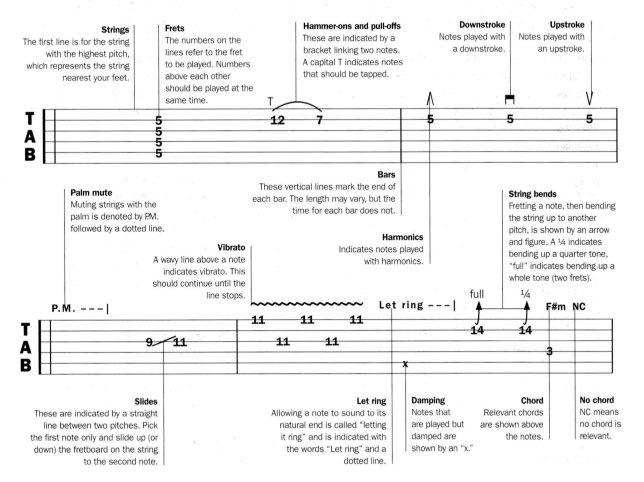

Strings
The first line is for the string with the highest pitch, which represents the string nearest your feet.

Frets
The numbers on the lines refer to the fret to be played. Numbers above each other should be played at the same time.

Hammer-ons and pull-offs
These are indicated by a bracket linking two notes. A capital T indicates notes that should be tapped.

Downstroke
Notes played with a downstroke.

Upstroke
Notes played with an upstroke.

Palm mute
Muting strings with the palm is denoted by P.M. followed by a dotted line.

Bars
These vertical lines mark the end of each bar. The length may vary, but the time for each bar does not.

String bends
Fretting a note, then bending the string up to another pitch, is shown by an arrow and figure. A ¼ indicates bending up a quarter tone, "full" indicates bending up a whole tone (two frets).

Vibrato
A wavy line above a note indicates vibrato. This should continue until the line stops.

Harmonics
Indicates notes played with harmonics.

Slides
These are indicated by a straight line between two pitches. Pick the first note only and slide up (or down) the fretboard on the string to the second note.

Let ring
Allowing a note to sound to its natural end is called "letting it ring" and is indicated with the words "Let ring" and a dotted line.

Damping
Notes that are played but damped are shown by an "x."

Chord
Relevant chords are shown above the notes.

No chord
NC means no chord is relevant.

Effects and
Accessories

Ever since Keith Richards used a fuzz box to create that famous opening riff in "Satisfaction," guitarists have been using effects and accessories to change or enhance the sound of the guitar. They can be great fun to experiment with, but don't feel you need to rush out and buy some. Many of the great Chicago bluesmen preferred nothing between their guitar and amp but a lead! However, if you want to copy or cover others, it's good to have a brief knowledge of how they've souped up their sound. Below you'll learn about the more commonly used effects and the type of sounds they can be used to create.

Effects

Distortion/Overdrive: From a sound that's mildly breaking up to saturated distortion, these are the thrilling rock tones that also aid legato playing.

Compressor/Limiter: These even out the sonic "highs" and "lows" to give you an even signal and control over the attack and decay of each note or interval, increasing the impression of sustain.

Echo, Reverb, or Delay: These simulate the acoustic ambience found in rooms or halls, or delay the signal, either with a short "slapback" or a longer decay.

Pitch Shifters: Octavers or harmonizers add notes to your signal, either an octave or two lower, or other key-specific intervals. Vibrato bars fitted to solid-body guitars are usually of the standard Strat design, or else lockable (featuring a lockable nut at the headstock too), such as a Kahler or Floyd Rose. Dramatic "whammy" effects can also be achieved with pedals, Tom Morello–style.

Wah wahs: Auto wahs and classic controllable wahs, such as the Cry Baby, allow for fast boosting or cutting of a particular frequency band (see page 181).

Modulation: Chorus and flanging both combine a slightly delayed signal with the original to create their characteristic thickening and shimmering effects. Phasing combines an out-of-phase signal with the original to create a sound as if your speaker were being spun around!

Tremolo: This varies the volume for a "wowing" or pulsating effect.

Noise suppressor/gate: Effects can add noise to the signal chain, so these simply mute the sound when you're not playing.

Accessories

Picks: Fingerstyle techniques are not just for acoustic—rockers like Jeff Beck have made great use of them. However, we'd suggest starting out with a pick to give yourself the choice—they vary between 0.5 and 2.0mm, with most people using a 0.75 or 1mm. Thicker picks are better for fast runs and shredding techniques.

Tuner: Even if you have a great ear and are a pro at tuning acoustically, spare your friends—and one day an audience—those familiar sounds.

Leads: It's worth investing in good leads by the likes of Whirlwind, Klotz, or Planet Waves. Cheap leads can reduce the signal path—and hence the tone. Even boutique effects pedals are only as good as the worst lead in your rig.

Metronome: Essential for phrase training, this teaches timing—speed it up on each exercise as you become more accurate. Many recording devices, drum machines, or software will also do this job.

Amplification

Back in the days of swing and big bands, the poor guitar player had nothing more than a small, low-powered amplifier to try and cut through the sound of all those horns. During the early 1960s, when bands such as the Beatles were struggling to be heard against thousands of screaming fans, a new kind of amp was born out of necessity, the high-powered 4x12 stack.

A guitar amp will usually consist of two elements: equalization (see our "Setting the Tone" panels later in the book), which is a combination of treble, middle, and bass; and gain and volume. Your volume is the master for the overall output, while the gain or drive control increases or decreases the degree to which that is saturated with an overdriven or distorted sound.

You may have come across the great valve/transistor debate. Valve amps are the real deal and have plenty of "mojo," whether bright and clean like a Fender Twin and Roland Jazz Chorus, or classically thumping like a Marshall. Transistor amps are usually as reliable as

Marshall amplifier
Known for great tone, reliability, and versatility, Marshall amps have been many players' favorites for decades.

a hammer in comparison, as valve amps need more frequent servicing and are as fragile as you'd expect anything using glass bottles containing a vacuum to be!

Classic valve amps need to be turned up to achieve their overloaded sound—as some guitarists must repeatedly explain to their neighbors. Until you're really sure you want to stick with the electric guitar, transistors are fine, but you will need at least 50 watts of transistor power if you want to compete with even a not-too-heavy drummer, and at least 15–20 watts of valve power. (Valves sound louder at the same rating.) An amp has pre-amp and power-amp stages, and some affordable "valvestate" amps go for a combination, with one stage featuring valves and the other transistors.

For the bedroom, however, there are now some great, no-frills valve practice amps, which, at around 5 watts, give you a great overdriven sound at home-stereo volume.

Channel switching allows you to swap between two or three "dirty" or "clean" (distorted or not) sounds in the same song. (You may want to check if the footswitch is included in the amp price.) Fender pioneered the inclusion of tremolo and spring reverb in guitar amps, but these days there's also a growing range of digital-modelling amps and combos, which include effects (and even different amp and cabinet simulations). These aren't real analogue effects, but computer simulations triggered by your playing. Nonetheless, they can be a great way of checking out what effects can do, if you don't own a load, or a "multi-FX," unit already.

Harmony and Melody

Now we're ready for the "business end"—getting started on the music. The aim of this chapter is to get you playing as quickly as possible, while also giving you enough theory to understand what you're doing as you go along, but not so much that it slows down your playing, as it's vital to hone your technique, too. All music consists of harmonic and melodic content. "Melody," of course, refers to the tune you are playing as it goes by real time—the one you could whistle or play on a monophonic (single-note) instrument. "Harmony" is where music really gets interesting: it refers to the interplay of the notes and the intervals between them. Whether these intervals are played as crashing, dramatic chord shapes (sounding all the notes at once) or arpeggiated (with the notes played one after another), the notes within the chord will be based on the same scale you arpeggiate.

Fender Jaguar
Fender's 1962 release, the Jaguar, quickly became a staple of the emerging surf music scene and became popular again in the 1990s with a number of grunge and alt rock bands, including Sonic Youth, Dinosaur Jr., Nirvana, and My Bloody Valentine.

Major and Minor
Scales

"Do, re, mi, fa, so, la, te, do"—the major scale may make you think more of *The Sound of Music* than the sound of rock music. But there have been plenty of killer solos played using the major and minor scales, so it's as important to have these scales at your fingertips as it is the Minor Pentatonic and the Minor Blues scales.

These scales are the essential building blocks of song structure, and how other scales and chords are built will be explained with reference to these. They are "true" scales, containing all seven notes until the tonic is naturally repeated, which just means it sounds the same to us, only higher—on the eighth note above—hence "octave."

The chromatic scale consists of all the twelve semitonal (half-step) notes that are physically possible—in other words, all the keys of a piano. By itself it is non-diatonic, which just means it has no key center because all the intervals (any two or more notes) are the same distance apart. Any scale picks out notes from this, and the major scale picks out in the following intervals:

tone—tone—semitone—tone—tone—tone—semitone

The natural minor scale differs in having a third note one semitone lower than the major scale—this one shift causes the biggest difference of mood between pieces of music. It is closely related to the pentatonic minor and minor blues scales (see pages 60 and 61).

> **"It was a joke, as far as I was concerned, I was just f****n' around when I came up with that riff."**
>
> *Slash* (Guns N' Roses) *on "Sweet Child Of Mine"*

TRACK 02/1

MAJOR SCALE
This diagram shows a movable major scale pattern with root on the E string. The tab shows a lower-register A-major scale.

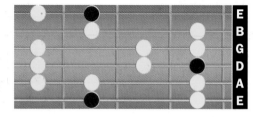

TRACK 02/2

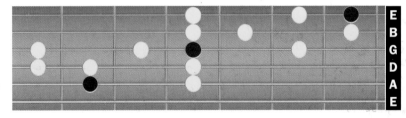

MAJOR SCALE

This diagram shows a movable major scale pattern with root on the A string. The tab shows a higher-register A-major scale.

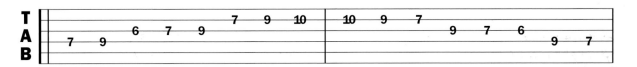

 TRACK 02/3

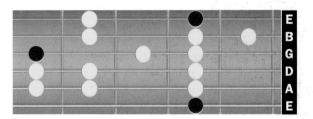

NATURAL MINOR BEGINNING ON THE E STRING

This diagram shows a movable natural minor scale pattern with root on the E string. The tab shows a lower-register E-minor scale.

 TRACK 02/4

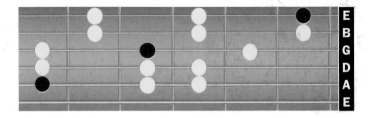

NATURAL MINOR

This diagram shows a movable natural minor scale pattern with root on the A string. The tab shows a higher-register A-minor scale.

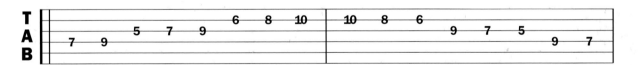

Open Chord
Shapes

Now that you've learned some scale patterns and warmed up your fingers, it's time to get into some chord shapes. Don't be put off if you find some of these shapes a little awkward at first—all your favorite players had to work to get these down. Practice them regularly and frequently and you'll be strumming away in no time!

We'll look at strumming and picking techniques on pages 26 and 27. But for now, make sure you are sounding each string, with a simple downstroke if necessary. As mentioned on page 14, concentrate on not damping the strings next to the ones you're fretting (unless indicated). Changing quickly between shapes is a big part of the rhythm or jazz guitarist's art, so although there's no need to play to a metronome while you are committing them to memory, you can work toward fast changes. In fact, there are times when it's simply great fun to improve your technique and not think about what you're playing.

Refer back to these chord charts as you work through the rest of the book. Unlike in tab, the numbers in the chord boxes represent the best finger to use. A red circle represents the tonic (root) note of the chord.

A zero at the left-hand side of the chord box illustrates that you play the open string beside it (a red zero indicates the root note). An "x" indicates that it is to be damped with the fretting hand. Practice angling your fretting finger slightly so that the side flesh of it is choking off any sound from that string. It sounds more tricky than it really is, and will become second nature after a while.

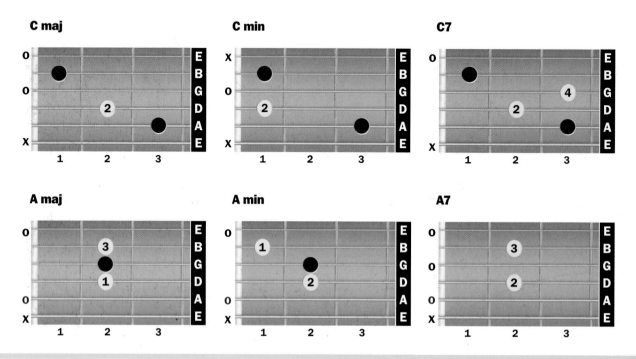

POPULAR CHORDS

Don't be put off by the number of chords here. They belong to the most popular keys for guitar-based music. You can dip back to these as you work through the exercises that follow. There is also a more advanced chord directory on pages 188–190 at the back of the book. Take time to practice the feel of the shapes your fretting hand makes for each chord.

> **"I'm not joking around when I've said occasionally [that] trying to learn how to play a D chord properly has been a very big thing for me."**
>
> *Lou Reed* on learning chords

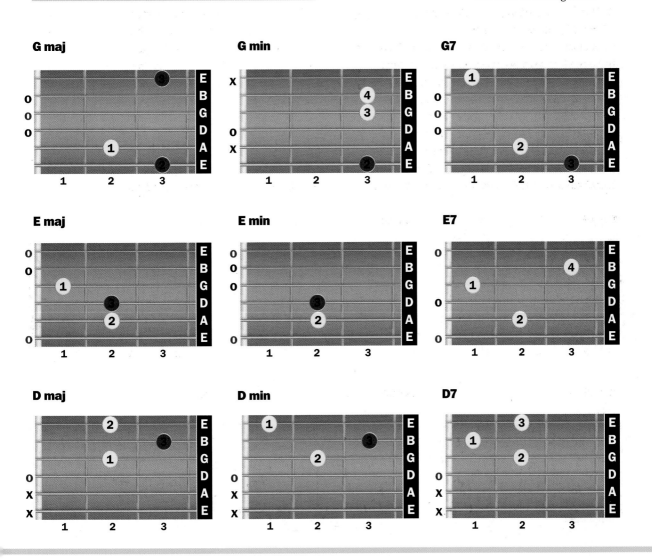

Strumming and
Picking Patterns

In this chapter you'll learn how to create an accompaniment with your new chord shapes. Strumming patterns and picking patterns are what guitarists use to base their accompaniments on. Done right, they create timeless, magical music; Jimmy Pages's intro for "Stairway to Heaven" is the perfect example of a great picking pattern.

PICKING

Anchor your hand, if needed, with your third and fourth fingers on the guitar's body, or else hold your hand above them, so that your plectrum (pick) is striking each string at the same angle. This will give evenness to your playing from the start, for which you may thank yourself later, as poor technique takes more conscious effort to fix than it does to learn. Avoid letting your wrist fall low relative to the strings. If you do, you may get into a habit of angling your wrist upward slightly which, however good you are, will slow you down.

You should be looking to have both a relaxed wrist and some movement in your thumb and forefinger. From your forearm to your fingertips, no part of your natural picking equipment should be locked rigid. Feel and sensitivity are the order of the day—you are not out to attack your axe, however much Slayer's Kerry King may look like he's doing just that!

You should find that you are moving up and down the strings at a 45-degree angle such that you are picking the higher strings (in pitch) slightly forward of the lower. Almost automatically, you will see that you can use the flat outer side of your left palm to damp all the strings at once, and you should find yourself capable of degrees of abrupt or gentle damping, including the gentle damped

Picking
Let your hand float above the strings rather than tethering it to a resting point on the guitar.

picking that sounds great with arpeggiated lines of the kind that Steve Cropper or Andy Summers play.

ALTERNATE PICKING

While picking straight down (in downstrokes) can sound edgy and punky as a contrived style in the hands of bands like The Offspring, it will not get you very far in any other context. "Alternate picking" simply refers to moving your thumb and forefinger back up once you have picked a string, picking the string for the second time with the uppermost side of your pick. This is an essential trick to master, allowing for the fluid and easy playing of the classic rock techniques, such as triplets and double-stops that feature later in the book.

STRUMMING

When it comes to an alternating technique, the same goes for strumming, or playing all of the strings at once.

The same principle of economizing your movement applies—on the downstroke, there's no need to take your pick too far below the top E string before bringing it back up for the upstroke.

Damping a strummed chord with the flat, soft outer flesh of your hand resting lightly across the strings where they meet the bridge, and playing downstrokes, has a sense of menace you may recognize from metal and rock songs, where it often occurs in the verse, building up the tension before a chorus or crescendo.

As you strum, you will find your fretting-hand damping techniques become more important for muting the strings that are not part of the chord. You should find yourself coordinating these almost unconsciously with the ability to damp all the strings with your strumming hand— leading to powers of total guitar control, at any level of gain and volume.

Strumming
A typical strumming motion where most of the movement comes from the wrist and hand.

Tempo and
Rhythm

Regular practice with a metronome will mean that your sense of timing will improve the more you play. There are two aspects to consider when it comes to keeping your chops and licks in time with the music, and it will help your compositional abilities if you keep the distinction in mind.

TEMPO

This refers to the pace of a piece of music and is measured in beats per minute (bpm). While DJs and dance-music producers often talk of bpm, and drum machines and sequencers allow you to dial in your choice of bpm right away, the concept derives from classical music. The scale of notational terms, from *largo* (solemnly slow) to *presto* (very fast), spans between 40 and 208 bpm, and in classical pieces it is up to the conductor to set the tempo.

In traditional rock music, one of a drummer's core skills is to set the most effective tempos for their songs. Music played too fast for its chosen style can utterly fail to convey the feelings intended in its harmonic content; too slow and even an interesting set of changes will seem dull and predictable enough to have audience members heading for the door. This can apply whether you are showcasing a prog rock concept album or playing in a nihilistic thrash metal band.

RHYTHM

It is as important to develop your sense of rhythm as it is to be in tune. A "tight" band that plays a few dud notes will be far more bearable than a band with one or more members who have an issue with staying in time. It's beyond the scope of this book to explain music in notational terms (although the music to the complete songs in the later chapters is presented in notation as well as tab for those who already read), but some key concepts in rock music are based on it.

One of these is the idea of the bar, simply a manageable "chunk" containing a certain number of beats that is consistent for that piece of music and is determined by the time signature. These are typically expressed as fractions in which the second (or bottom) number refers to the time value of the beat and the first (or top) to the number of beats within the bar. Hence, "four-four time" refers to there being four beats in a bar. A piece of music in two-four (2/4) time will therefore have double the number of bars as a piece of music of the same length in four-four (4/4) time. As you learn, you will come to instantly recognize the difference in feel between them.

Besides these two time signatures, the third most common is three-four (3/4), or "waltz" time, rare in rock but dramatic when it occurs, as in Jimi Hendrix's

> ❝When you sit down and think about what rock 'n' roll music really is, then you have to change that question. Played up-tempo, you call it rock 'n' roll; at a regular tempo, you call it rhythm and blues.❞
>
> **Little Richard** *on the effects of tempo*

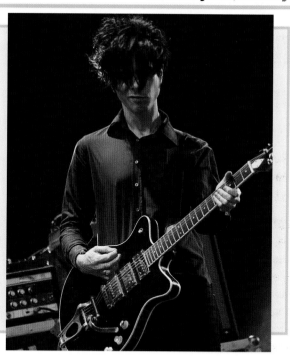

"Manic Depression." These time signatures, based on triple, duple, or quadruple time, are known as simple time signatures to distinguish them from compound time signatures, where the value of each beat will be a multiple of two, four, or three (such as six-eight time, with six beats in the bar, where each beat is one eighth note).

By now you will have realized that beats are distinct from notes. Any group of notes or rests (where no note in that instrument's part is played on the given beat[s]) can be played in a bar as long as their total time value is consistent with the time value of the number of beats in the bar.

The dynamism of a piece of music derives precisely from the interplay between its individual parts, from whether or not they play on any given beat (or between them). Syncopation (deviation from the pulse beat, in many ways common to swing, blues, jazz, and rock) and anacrusis (a specific syncopation in which you begin a part in advance of a bar—"*And…one..,*" which is common to many vocal lines) are just two examples of dynamic playing and composition. Similarly, the division of a piece of music into its constituent bars may or may not bear relation to where its repeated (*ostinato*) phrases or riff cycles occur, although it very often does. When musicians say cryptically that what they don't play is as important as the notes they do play, this is what they have in mind.

TIME VALUES

American notation	Classical notation	No. per bar
Whole note	semibreve	1
Half note	minim	2
Quarter note	crotchet	4
Eighth note	quaver	8
Sixteenth note	semiquaver	16

The corresponding fractions apply to rests (a direction *not* to play), so that you will hear reference to, for example, a whole-note rest.

We'll look at triplets (groups of three notes in which each note is stressed the same way, with the same time value) on pages 100 and 101.

Simple Movable
Chord Shapes

Movable chord shapes are the staples of fast, easy, and effective pop song composition, especially in punky, alternative genres. Major or minor, happy or sad, they provide the budding guitarist with a quick way to vary their chord voicings (positions). They can be learned and deployed effectively and visually without knowing all the theory behind them at first, which will help you learn the theory from the inside out while you have some fun and are already playing convincingly. The following is far from an exhaustive list of movable chord shapes. Fretting a barre with your index finger may seem daunting at first. If so, remember that you're not the only one who's found it so. Perseverance and practice will pay off.

Later in the book, we'll take a look at movable chord shapes featuring some of the more complex secondary intervals that jazz and funk guitarists use, as well as more complex fingerings. We will also examine chord shapes that are movable against open strings that

are being used as "drone" or pedal notes—a folk and psychedelic favorite. But for that, we need a little more knowledge of key signatures.

No frets are marked on these diagrams, as movable chords can be played, as the name suggests, at any fret.

Major barre chords with root on the E string:

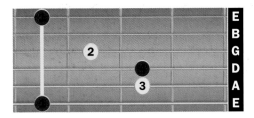

Major barre chords with root on the A string:

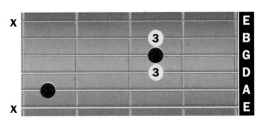

Minor barre chords with root on the E string:

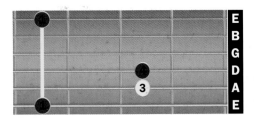

Minor barre chords with root on the A string:

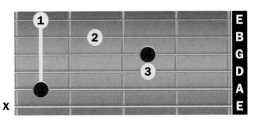

**Barre seventh chords
with root on the E string:**

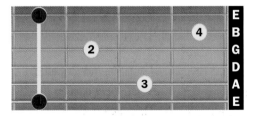

**Barre seventh chords
with root on the A string:**

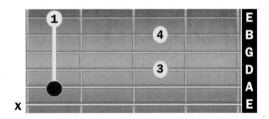

**Minor seventh barre chords
with root on the E string:**

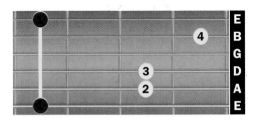

**Minor seventh barre chords with
root on the A string:**

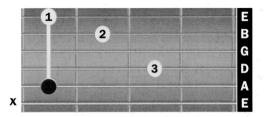

**Barre major seventh chords
with root on the A string:**

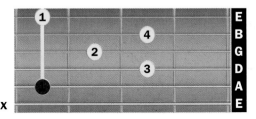

**Major seventh chords
with root on the E string:**

**Alternative major barre chords
with root on the E string:**

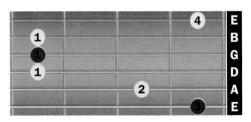

**Alternative major barre chords
with root on the A string:**

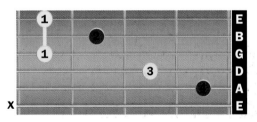

Keys and
Modulation

The mysterious language of keys looks at first like pure mathematics but is best understood as being based on the natural behavior of sound. In our culture, the tonal center of a piece of music can be described in terms of a major or minor scale, and is determined by the tonic triad—a group of three notes, in this case the first, third, and fifth, of this scale. Only certain chords will sound right when built on each note of this scale (see page 22).

For example, a song played in C major would consist of some or all of the following chords: C, Dm, Em, F, G, Am, B°. The last one, built upon B as the seventh of C, is a diminished chord, which is to say it has a flattened fifth as well as a flattened third. As you jam around with the chords you are learning from pages 24, 25, 30, and 31, you will hear how some sound tense and some sound resolved and calm. Chords such as those built on the fifth of each scale sound intrinsically like they should resolve to the tonic. This tension gives music its sense of motion.

The sixth chord in a key built on the major scale is also important because it gives us the tonic chord of the relative minor scale: you will see from the chart opposite that each major key has a relative minor that repeats the same chords from the sixth note onward as its relative major. This means that either C major or A minor pentatonic scale patterns (see pages 60 and 64) can sound great when played against these chords. Not only that, but great guitarists will betray their awareness, in the solos and lines they play, of each underlying chord or imply the chords if they're the only guitarist, using the notes of the chords as they occur as well as sticking to the scale overall.

A knowledge of keys is essential—for composition, of course, but also when preparing to play with instruments limited to one key, such as harmonica (or harp, in the Blues), or the instrument you are most likely to play with that will sound much better in some keys than others—the human voice.

Playing the same piece of music in different keys is known as "transposition," and you will also use it to make pieces easier to play or more effective, tailoring the key to facilitate your tricks for a certain style, such as whether or not you like to make use of open strings as pedal notes without retuning your guitar.

Jimi Hendrix
Adept at using key changes to maximum effect, Jimi Hendrix's anthemic guitar solos and masterful playing made him a rock legend and guitar icon.

Keys and key signatures may differ slightly—a song or other composition will have an overall key signature but may contain more than one key. Where this occurs it's known as "modulation." Pop and rock songs especially contain very simple modulations, a common compositional trick to increase excitement, which feature in the final verse of many hits. It can be quite corny when done obviously, but also effective if well deployed.

For example, you might have a typical progression featuring E, B, D, and A (in the key of E). A third verse or section that featured F#, C#, E, and B would represent a typical pop/rock trick of modulating the whole piece by a whole tone. Ending the second progression on the B, as the fifth (dominant) of E, would allow you to resolve naturally to the E—either to end on the tonic, or return to your first pattern in the key of E.

Key Chord Chart

MAJOR KEY

 # = SHARP   **° = DIMINISHED**

I	II	III	IV	V	VI	VII
A	Bm	C#m	D	E	F#m	G#°
B	C#m	D#m	E	F#	G#m	A#°
C	Dm	Em	F	G	Am	B°
D	Em	F#m	G	A	Bm	C#°
E	F#m	G#m	A	B	C#m	D#°
F	Gm	Am	B♭	C	Dm	E°
G	Am	Bm	C	D	Em	F#°

MINOR KEY

DARKER COLUMNS DENOTE THE RELATIVE MINOR

I	II	III	IV	V	VI	VII
Am	B°	C	Dm	Em	F	G
Bm	C#°	D	Em	F#m	G	A
Cm	D°	E♭	Fm	Gm	A♭	B♭
Dm	E°	F	Gm	Am	B♭	C
Em	F#°	G	Am	Bm	C	D
Fm	G°	A♭	B♭m	Cm	D♭	E♭
Gm	A°	B♭	Cm	Dm	E♭	F

Arpeggiating Chords
with a Pick

"Arpeggio" is a big word for a simple concept, which refers to playing the notes of a chord in sequence rather than sounding them at once. For example, in a passage of music with a single chord change per bar, you would highlight the individual notes of the chord over each beat (see pages 28–29)—or half, quarter—of the bar.

Arpeggiating chords in rhythm parts is a great way to add contrast and dynamics to your music. They're great for anticipatory passages leading into that fist-in-the-air, power chord–driven chorus, or for styles of music that don't make a feature of the "question and answer" quality that chords followed by licks have.

They feature heavily, therefore, in post-punk and pop guitar styles, where delay and modulation effects—such as Andy Summers used on "Message in a Bottle" by The Police—helped to distance them further from the traditional rock tones of the time. Meanwhile, mixing arpeggiated chords with strummed chords is a staple of laid-back pop picking, often with a bright Telecaster or Rickenbacker tone.

While popular with fingerstyle players, arpeggios are also a gift for your picking hand, since they can be played smoothly and evenly with downstrokes, and also lend themselves to damping (damped arpeggios with saturated distortion are a popular feature of metal). Thinking in terms of arpeggios can also be a great help for lead-guitar passages. But in overall compositional terms, following the exercises below should give an insight into

ARPEGGIATING COMPLEX CHORDS
Try to avoid the temptation to arpeggiate those hard-to-fret complex chords simply as a substitute for practicing on-the-beat changes with them.

 **TRACK 03**

EXERCISE I
A straightforward F#5/G#5/A5 progression with a flowing 1980's-style arpeggiated picking pattern.

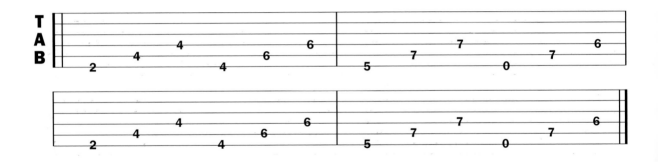

Andy Summers
In The Police's hit "Every Breath You Take," guitarist Summers weaves a rich backdrop, arpeggiating chord voicings and creating an unforgettable sound.

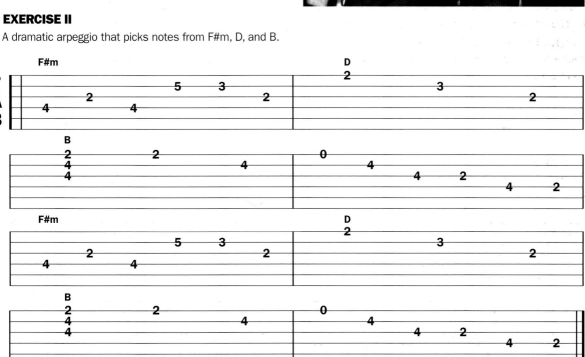

how riffs are also derived from them. Once you have arpeggiated some of the barre chords found on pages 30 and 31, you'll see that it's not a big leap to add passing notes from scales outside of the arpeggiated chords, making for an interesting interval that could be the basis of a brand-new riff.

 **TRACK 04**

EXERCISE II

A dramatic arpeggio that picks notes from F#m, D, and B.

Sweep
Picking

We saw on page 27 how alternate picking (and, for that matter, strumming) increases the number of given notes your picking hand can play in any given length of time. Sweep picking builds on this technique and is the secret behind the lightning-fast salvos fired by lead players such as Slayer's Kerry King.

It's an advanced technique included here since it's often used in tandem with arpeggios. Don't worry if you feel you won't master it swiftly—you can return to this technique when you're ready.

FRETTING
Your fretting-hand technique should remain even; this is not a blues- or rhythm guitar-style technique featuring string damping or other finger contortions in which your fretting-hand position may need to change. So keep an even pressure from your thumb on the back of the neck, as the following exercises require some precision.

TRACK 05

Whereas alternate picking can be applied to any set of notes, sweep picking depends on having a particular fretting-hand pattern in mind, and although described as a picking technique, it involves close coordination with your fretting hand too. It will, however, allow you to move from string to string very fast. For this reason, it's generally used for arpeggios, since it is played to best effect the fewer the notes there are per individual string.

In the following exercises, you will notice how the picking is organized so that an odd number of strokes on each string takes you in the same direction across them that you began the phrase with, and with an even number, you reverse direction: begin them on an upstroke. When sweep picking, you may find you have a natural desire to speed up when you come to a part you sweep rather than other alternately picked parts—be sure to keep the tempo even all along. Page 132 will show you how to incorporate sweep picking with a simple picking-hand tapping technique.

EXERCISE I
An Amaj7 arpeggio in a fretting pattern for sweep picking.

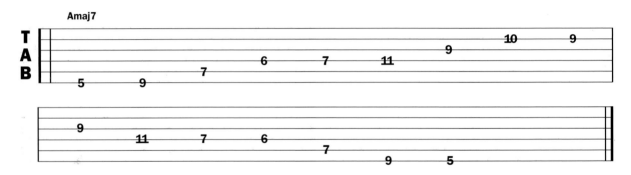

Joe Satriani
Satriani has augmented his solo career playing with performers such as Alice Cooper, Mick Jagger, Deep Purple, and Chickenfoot. A rock guitar virtuoso, "Satch" is a master of speed-related techniques such as rapid alternate picking and sweep picking.

 **TRACK 06**

EXERCISE II

Dmaj7 arpeggio—another workout for your fretting hand.

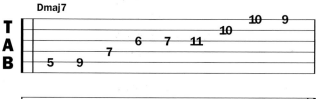

 **TRACK 07**

EXERCISE III

Bmin7 picking pattern that could be used in a solo.

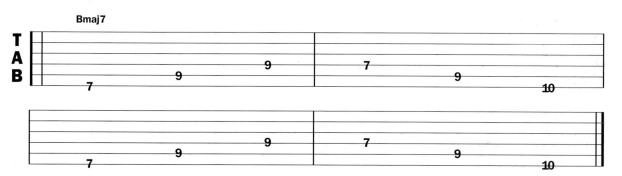

Play
Riffs

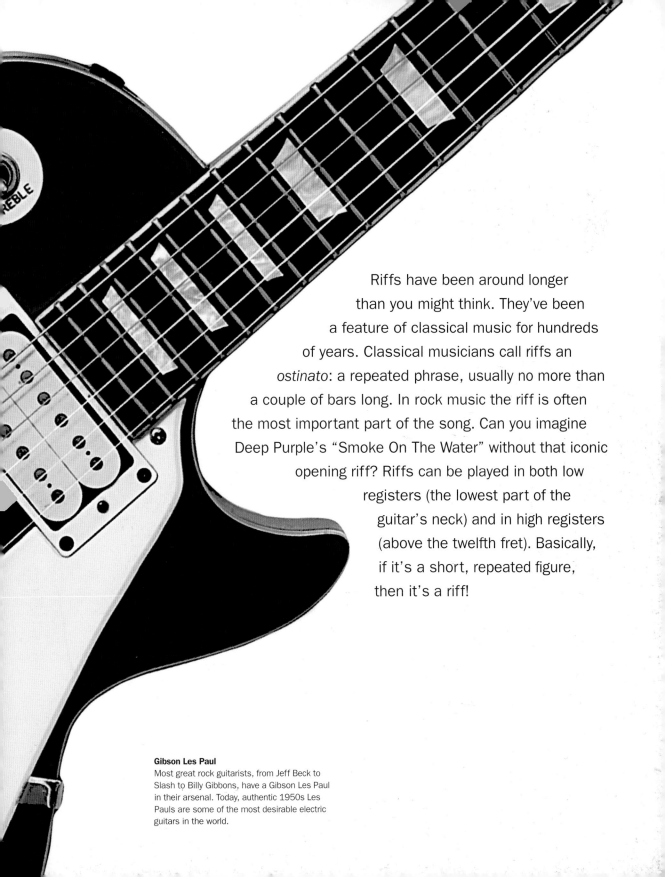

Riffs have been around longer
than you might think. They've been
a feature of classical music for hundreds
of years. Classical musicians call riffs an
ostinato: a repeated phrase, usually no more than
a couple of bars long. In rock music the riff is often
the most important part of the song. Can you imagine
Deep Purple's "Smoke On The Water" without that iconic
opening riff? Riffs can be played in both low
registers (the lowest part of the
guitar's neck) and in high registers
(above the twelfth fret). Basically,
if it's a short, repeated figure,
then it's a riff!

Gibson Les Paul
Most great rock guitarists, from Jeff Beck to
Slash to Billy Gibbons, have a Gibson Les Paul
in their arsenal. Today, authentic 1950s Les
Pauls are some of the most desirable electric
guitars in the world.

Single-Note
Riffs

While you're learning to play, it's important to create some pleasant noises from your guitar at least every once in a while. Reward yourself with some of these, and they will keep you sitting there through the hours of practicing fast chord changes or while learning any of the other techniques that everyone struggles with at first.

Single-note riffs will put a smile on your face! Once you can fret and pick notes smoothly and without buzz, you can play brooding, stirring riffs that are garage-band standards, and in that context will make you sound as good as someone who's been playing for years.

Of course single-note riffs are not purely melodic—they will have harmonic content when played against a bass line in the context of a band. Try the following exercises on their own, and then against a recording of a bass line (which can be played on your six-string for these purposes) consisting of the root note of each chord. You will see how classic riffs often use passing notes, typically from the pentatonic or minor blues scales.

> **"Don't be afraid to screw up! One of the key issues to learning is making mistakes . . . if you're not making mistakes, you're probably not having a very good time".**
>
> **Robben Ford** *on learning to play guitar*

 **TRACK 08**

EXERCISE I
This E5 classic-rock riff shows how riffs can be built from the pentatonic. Aim for an accurate hammer-on and quarter-tone string bend (see page 55).

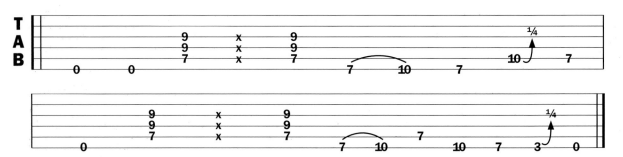

Jimmy Page

One of the most influential guitarists in rock 'n' roll, Jimmy Page was the founding member of Led Zeppelin and, previously, a member of The Yardbirds. He was one of the first guitarists to help popularize the use of electronic feedback and distortion with the Roger Mayer fuzzbox. As a producer, composer, and guitarist for Led Zep, Page became one of the major driving forces behind the rock sound of that era. With his trademark Gibson Les Paul and Marshall amp, his use of distorted fuzz guitar—as heard on "Whole Lotta Love"—Page made Led Zep a prototype for all future rock bands.

 **TRACK 09**

EXERCISE II

A simple poppy riff in D. The CD track will indicate timing.

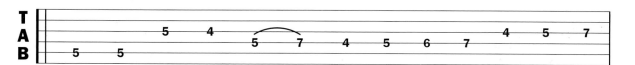

 **TRACK 10**

EXERCISE III

A moody riff in C that can be against the chords Am, G, D, or C (see page 175).

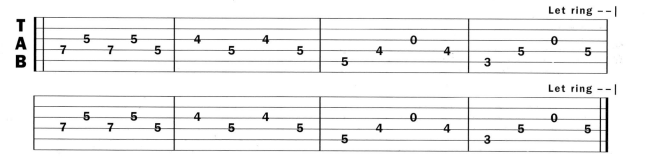

Double-Stop
Riffs

Broadly speaking, a double stop is simply two notes played at the same time, or very close together. We will take a look at some of their uses when soloing on page 99. But double-stop phrases are ideal for riffing, as they can be used to imply the chords, keeping the tonal center established in riffs that consist of single-note phrases as well.

Playing double-stops is also ideal for those times when the guitar is not the lead instrument—for example, when a singer is letting rip in the middle of a verse—but you still want to contribute something a little more imaginative than simply vamping the music's underlying chords.

Harmonically, double-stops can be used to emphasize the particular intervals inherent in a chord progression. Using the information from pages 32 and 33, you will find that the feel of the chords built on the intervals of the major or minor scales in any given key will be influenced by the intervals within them.

Convention: In discussion of tab and musical composition, Arabic numerals—1, 2, 3, etc.—indicate

the note of the scale; Roman numerals—I, IV, V, etc.—indicate the chords built on each note. An instruction to play any particular Roman chord of any major or minor key will carry with it the implication to play its tonality, in which, for example, the second chord is always minor, etc. See the chart on page 33 if you're in any doubt as to what these are.

In the following exercises, you should see how the interval of each double-stop helps to establish the mood of the riff—as sweeter or more assertive, for example, according to whether the third (which establishes major or minor harmony) or the fifth (which is not called the dominant for nothing) are used.

TRACK 11/1

EXERCISE I

A rocky double-stop riff in B. A strong fourth finger is needed for the slide in the second bar.

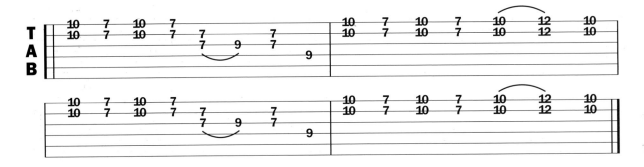

Double-stop

The basic effect of playing double-stops is of harmonizing with your solo playing. This technique was used by many lead guitarists in bands of the fifties and sixties. Rock 'n' roll legend Chuck Berry was a champion of double-stop playing, using them in nearly every song, including the rock 'n' roll classics "Johnny Be Goode," and "Roll over Beethoven."

Chuck Berry
There is little doubt that Chuck Berry's "Maybellene"—combining blues and country music with teenager-aimed lyrics and smoking electric guitar solos—was one of the first major examples of the rock 'n' roll form.

 **TRACK 11/2**

EXERCISE II

A classic-sounding minor-to-major power-chord riff. This requires careful damping.

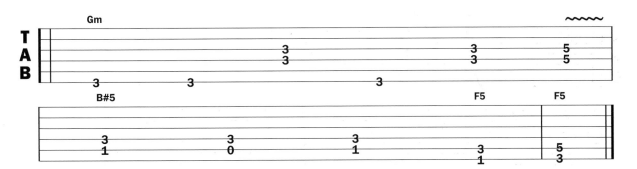

Power Chord
Riffs

Barre chords produce a surprising amount of tone color—too much for some purposes, especially when the music at hand is out to take as bold and decisive a tone as a lot of rock music. If you're looking to make a confident, strident statement without the ambiguity and reflectiveness of major or minor tonalities, then power-chord riffs are the way to go.

Power chords are not about the notes that go into them but about the ones left out. Since they do not have a third, they are neither major nor minor, but contain just the tonic and the dominant, which together make an assertive rock 'n' roll statement.

The following ways of playing power chords provide you with movable chord shapes that are the basis of many riffs. Having no extended harmonic tensions to resolve, you can change key fast in a power chord–driven piece of music. The fingerings, which involve the first or first and third fingers, are easy diad (two-note) shapes that allow for maximum mobility on the fretboard.

For this reason, power-chord riffs have been favorites of single-guitar bands including Led Zeppelin and

Black Sabbath. They can provide a solid basis for solo passages that intersperse them and even appear in solos themselves.

POWER CHORDS
Power chords are more flexible than barre chords when it comes to using them with an open string as a pedal note, as featured in the second exercise. They respond well to overdrive and distortion, whereas a chord with a third in it can often be muddy and dissonant, owing to the extra harmonics that fuzz effects can generate. So give these some gain and get riffing!

TRACK 12/1

EXERCISE I
A strident power-chord riff that uses the unexpected F5 in the third bar
(built on the minor sixth of the tonic key) to generate interest.

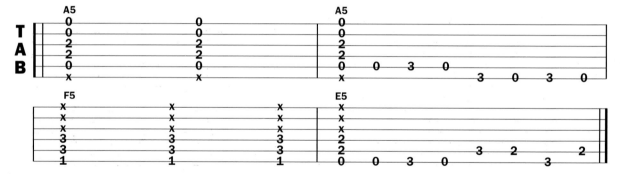

Power Chord Power

The simple ratios between the harmonics in the notes of a power chord give the stark, powerful sounds popularized by early heavy metal bands, such as Black Sabbath, Led Zeppelin, and Deep Purple. However, in 1964 The Kinks's song "You Really Got Me" became a hit built around power chords—clearly demonstrating the fast chord changes that would become typical of heavy rock riffs.

Tony Iommi
Some say that heavy metal would not exist without Tony Iommi. With ground-breaking heavy metal band Black Sabbath, his mighty guitar riffs and bone-crushing solos have defined the genre.

 TRACK 12/2

EXERCISE II

This riff uses ninths for a contemporary twist on power chord riffs. Despite these color notes, the chords remain ambiguous in their tonality without thirds.

```
        Dadd9        Eadd9        Cadd9
                                             0         3         0         3
T                                                      3                   3
   |  5          7          3                 2        0         2         0
A  |  7          9          5                 2        0         2         0
B  |  7          9          5                 0                  0
      5          7          3                          3                   3


        Dadd9        Eadd9        Cadd9
                                             0         3         0         3
                                                      3                   3
      5          7          3                 2        0         2         0
      7          9          5                 2        0         2         0
      7          9          5                 0                  0
      5          7          3                          3                   3
```

Barre Chord Riffs

You'll recognize barre-chord riffs right away as a staple of rock ballads, or as the more driving inspiration behind classic punk and post-punk tunes. Nonetheless, practice is required to become proficient at fretting sequences of barre chords. Sliding your barred first finger up and down all of the frets of the fretboard without buzz is not easy. You will play more cleanly and in time if you fret a series of barre chords staccato style, damping them as you raise your fingers from the frets simultaneously, sliding your fretting hand over your untensioned strings as it damps them, only fretting again in time with your strumming-hand stroke on the first beat where the next chord position occurs.

Similarly, you'll find your playing benefits from a tight level of rhythmic coordination between your right and left hands. Many players keep up a "phantom" rhythmic movement to mark time, maintaining the action of their strumming hand without their pick coming into contact with the strings. This technique will not only keep you in time but allows some great rhythmic, damped down- and up-strokes in which the notes are unfretted, which can help to syncopate a passage of music by accenting particular beats of the bar. (In this book, these are marked in tab as vertical lines of crosses across all six strings.)

The following riffs are constructed from the chords featured on pages 24 and 25. If you compare the intervals in these chords with the notes of the major or minor scales featured on pages 22 and 23, beginning on any root note, you will see that, besides the tonic, they also contain the major or minor third, together with the dominant. In the following exercise, the use of the second and third chords of the scale add a reflective element, while the fifth fulfills its dominant function of leading the ear back to the tonic chord. By utilizing each string, barre chords create a wide aural spectrum of notes, from low

TRACK 13

EXERCISE I

The D major chord built on the minor third of the root scale (B) gives this up-tempo riff its punky flavor. Fretting-hand damping will keep the chords staccato.

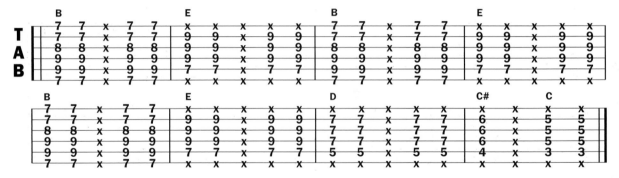

Steve Jones

Sex Pistols guitarist Steve Jones, who also played with Thin Lizzy, Joan Jett, Bob Dylan, Iggy Pop, and Megadeth, has been praised for precise and impeccable playing. The Pistols's only officially released studio recording, 1977's "Never Mind the Bollocks, Here's the Sex Pistols," is considered one of rock's all-time great recordings, and Jones's memorable guitar riffs colored many classic punk anthems, such as "Anarchy in the U.K.," "God Save the Queen," and "Pretty Vacant."

to high pitch, spanning three octaves. In the guitar-friendly keys of E and A (or with a capo or an alternative tuning), the tip of the index finger should cover the tonic note on the lowest string, and an open string can be used as a repeating bass "pedal" note that the barre chords cycle around.

TRACK 14

EXERCISE II

An upbeat new-wave riff over two cycles (see page 175). The I–V–VI–IV progression reasserts the fifth at the end of the second half.

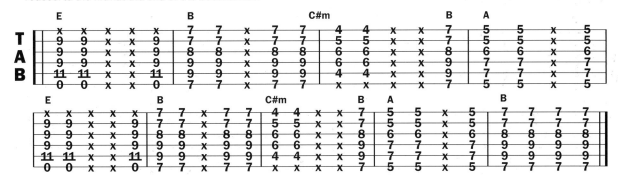

Chord
Inversions

As we saw on page 30, the different positions in which the same chord can be played are known as "voicings." Some voicings are known as "inversions." These are where the order of notes in the scale from which the chord is drawn are played in a different order from their usual of lowest to highest (or highest to lowest on an upstroke) in pitch, giving the chord a different bass note from its tonic.

Inversions are conventionally applied to triads—the first, third, and fifth of the scale. Major and minor triads span a perfect fifth—it's the third, in the middle, that defines the tonality. If you raise the tonic by an octave (this note is called the "unison"), it gives you the first inversion, with the third in the bass. Raise the third an octave and you have the fifth in the bass—the second inversion. Repeat once again and you are "back" to the root-position triad an octave higher.

Although some guitarists, like Alan Holdsworth, are known for their longer-than-average fingerspans, the typical human hand will only span so far along the fretboard. Inverting riffs in the same manner as triads can provide a way to include notes of the chord and

introduce the way they feel, harmonically, whereas an impossibly long finger stretch, or impossible chord shape, would preclude it. They also introduce a different sense of motion—by having a different bass line, as the root is no

WHAT YOU SHOULD AIM FOR
Despite the fretboard not being linear like a keyboard, your long-term goal should be to familiarize yourself with all the note positions along the fretboard and across all strings in standard (or your most-frequently used) tuning. Arpeggiated exercises are a great way to work toward that.

 **TRACK 15**

EXERCISE I
The inverted chords (C6/9 and G9) below add an expansive tone and descending bass line.

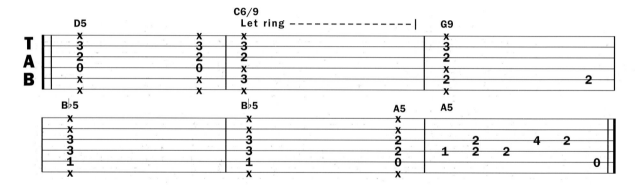

Malcolm Young
Malcolm Young is the co-founder and rhythm guitarist of the Australian hard rock band AC/DC. He and his brother Angus founded AC/DC in 1973. Influenced by '50s rock and roll and blues-based rock guitarists of the '60s and '70s, he is regarded as a leading rock exponent of rhythm guitar. His economic playing, his "groove," and his riff-based compositions have been highly influential on subsequent hard rock acts.

longer the tonic—from the notes if played in their conventional voicing in pitch order.

Barre chords with their root on the A string, together with chord voicings, such as inversions that often require a middle string to be damped, require practice. Removing your fingers from the frets while keeping them in contact with the strings allows you to move smoothly between chords.

 TRACK 16

EXERCISE II

The first inversion of C in the following riff makes for an easy transition from the preceding B♭5.

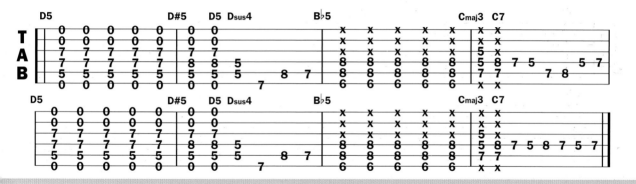

Fast and Furious
Riffs

Super-fast metal guitar playing may be a hallmark of today's bands such as Dragonforce and Trivium, but it has a longer history than that. Since the punk explosion, musicians have worked to fuse its energy and speed with the musicality of metal. In the intervening years, locking, super-accurate tremolo systems, and high-gain saturated distortion tones have made several devastating lead techniques easier to play smoothly. Today's neoclassical legato techniques and super-fast tempos often sound as if Randy Rhoads and Rat Scabes (drummer of legendary punks The Damned) were playing in the same band.

There are tips, tricks, and cheats that make super-fast riffing easier than it sounds. Pay attention to your string gauges—for tone, heavier is best, but .9s are easier to fret. Rhythm parts and riffs may often require you to pick diad intervals, or three notes at most—and if they don't, you are justified in simplifying them.

It's important with all material, of course, but especially with this style to begin your practice slowly and gradually speed your metronome to the desired tempo. The faster you play, the greater the temptation to gloss over the fingerings you feel are most difficult, as if shortcomings won't be heard come the day you perform your material. If you fail to establish your intended harmony, it will be perceptible in the quality of your performance, whether or not it's over in seconds.

FAST PLAYING

When it comes to playing fast, less is more, since a tight picking-hand technique is especially required to keep in time with the busy, sixteenth-note patterns of drummers who use two bass (kick) drums, for example.

 **TRACK 17**

EXERCISE I

The fast triad run in the first bar, played against the fifth of the chord, creates the illusion that you are moving the whole power chord.

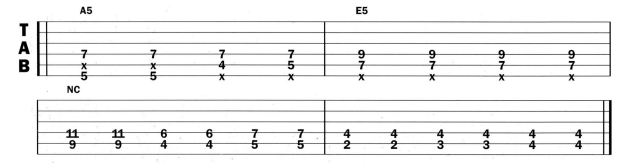

Fast Eddie Clarke
Motörhead's blistering guitarist between 1976 and 1982, Fast Eddie Clarke helped write dozens of the band's classic songs. *Ace of Spades* has been described as "one of the best metal albums by any band, ever" and has become a hugely influential hard rock classic. The album, and particularly its title track—a definitive Motörhead anthem—are considered among the most influential in the development of thrash metal.

Crank up your gain for the following exercises and see how single-note runs can be combined with power chords. This makes it easier to move quickly to a subsequent chord than a series of chord changes would allow, while still suggesting their implicit harmony. Note how playing fast lends itself to the use of chromatic (semitonal) runs and passing notes (notes with a very small time value) from outside the key.

 **TRACK 18**

EXERCISE II

Many songs contrast a strong power-chord chorus of ambiguous tonality with a verse consisting of major and/or minor chords, or vice versa, as in the following exercise. Play the second half in a shuffle rhythm (see page 76).

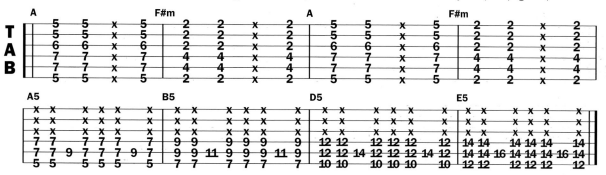

Play Solos

In the swing era of the 1930s and '40s, the guitarist's job was simply to play rhythm—it was the horn players who took the solos and got all the attention. However, with the growing use of the magnetic pickup, guitarists were able to amplify their semi-acoustic guitars and could finally compete with horn players for soloing space. Charlie Christian was one of the first guitarists to use this new technology; it freed him from the confines of being merely a rhythm player and allowed him to play solo lines that could be heard above the sound of a full big band.

Put simply, a solo is a passage of lead-guitar music, mostly melodic in content, but (with double-stops and other intervals) harmonic at times too. For the purposes of the following chapter, let's assume you are planning to solo with a band, or against a recording of one. The following suggestions take into account the need to sound in tune with rhythm guitar and/or bass parts, and the harmonic factors that will be constant. You will find, when you are practicing by yourself, that you have far more harmonic, and therefore melodic, freedom—a greater degree of notes will be available to you without their sounding dissonant.

Fender Stratocaster
The Strat's three single-coil pickups originally had the output selected by a three-way switch. Guitarists soon discovered that jamming the switch between the first and second positions selected the bridge and middle pickups, and second and third positions, the middle and neck pickups. The tone of the middle and bridge pickups was popularized by David Gilmour, Mark Knopfler, Bob Dylan, and Eric Clapton.

Hammer-ons and
Pull-offs

Along with string-bends and vibrato, hammer-ons and pull-offs are part of the trinity of essential lead-guitar techniques that every player needs to know. They are a method of generating a tone from a single string without using your picking hand and rely on strong first and third fingers. When playing fast runs it's difficult to fret every note cleanly, and even good players will admit you have to be very, very good to execute clean, fast runs where every note is picked. Hammering on and pulling off will let you complete runs without picking every note, giving fluid and smooth *legato* (sustained-note) playing.

Hammer-ons and pull-offs are mirror images of the same technique. In each case, you use the first finger of your fretting hand as an anchor point.

Hammering on: Rotate your wrist slightly in a circular motion and fret the note a whole tone above any fret on the G, B, or E strings at which you have just picked a note. Hammer on with your third finger. Without picking it, you should find that the higher note sustains thanks to the impact of your finger just behind the fret.

Pulling off: This is almost the reverse motion, except that instead of simply removing your third finger, pull it slightly downward as it leaves the upper fret, sounding the note that your index finger is still fretting.

Hammer-ons and pull-offs are executed individually in melodic phrases, while repeating the action is known as "trilling," a trick much used by guitarists to build a sense of expectation. You can hammer on with your second, third, or fourth fingers, meaning that you can apply the technique to widely spaced intervals—wider still when combined with tapping techniques (see page 132).

TRACK 19/1

Hammer-ons and pull-offs can be achieved anywhere on the neck, but practice high at first and there will be more definition to your notes. Get as much weight as you can behind your third finger while maintaining its accuracy.

Practice this at low gain and you will be pleasantly surprised at how much easier it becomes when you do turn up to eleven! Adding vibrato (see page 58) to a hammered-on note will really help to sustain it.

> **"Just because you know umpteen billion scales, it doesn't mean you have to use them all in a solo."**
>
> *Kirk Hammett* (Metallica)

TRACK 19/2

In all cases and at all speeds, practice keeping your tempo even between picked, hammered-on, and pulled-off notes, whether playing triplets (see page 101), eighth or sixteenth notes, or hammering and pulling individual phrases within your lead lines.

String Bends
and Slides

Bending strings is the heart and soul of blues-guitar playing. As the guitar moved away from being the "vamping" rhythm instrument of swing music and acoustic (Delta) blues, players began to emulate the lead lines of horn players. Trumpets, cornets, clarinets, and saxophones are instruments known for their smooth *glissando* sounds, in which one note glides into the next. Think of the opening bars of Gershwin's "Rhapsody in Blue" or John Coltrane's be-bop tenor-sax solos. These are the sounds that influenced the early lead-guitar players of electric blues.

There are two aspects to learn if you're to master these highly expressive playing skills and use them wisely: technique and judgement. String bends in particular should not be used indiscriminately. If a solo doesn't sound great then, assuming it's smoothly played, it's probably the case that a bend is obscuring rather than enhancing the harmonic structure—the whole- and half-tones (semitones) that establish the scale—introducing an unwanted chromatic element (otherwise known as a bum note).

Whether you are playing with a clean or dirty tone, practice sliding as evenly as possible at any speed, though in a solo it's likely that your slides themselves—not necessarily the notes they help to sustain—will last no longer than a couple of beats. Most are quick and impactful, whether ascending or descending. Slides come into their own when, as with a hammer-on, you use them to sound the second note without picking, sustaining it with the pressure of your fretting finger as it comes to a stop and, in all likelihood, applying vibrato.

TRACK 20/1

SLIDE I

Slides and bends make a similar glissando sound but are very different techniques. You will typically use the tips of your first and third fingers to slide between notes on the same string.

TRACK 20/2

SLIDE II

An ascending slide is a bold statement in a blues solo (used often by players such as B.B. King): pick the first note gently, emphasizing the second instead with the pressure of your finger as it comes to a stop. Using your first finger for a slide means that you have the freedom to fan out from your destination note with the other three, hammering on, pulling off, or picking from a wide choice of intervals.

STRING BENDS

Bending strings, meanwhile, is an ability that made keyboard players jealous enough to invent the pitch wheel. From a subtle technique involving quarter-tone bends, to wide intervals for "off the wall" sounds, string bends will take your playing to a whole new level of dynamics. Common bends other than the gentle quarter-tone include a half-tone, whole tone, and whole-and-a-half tone. For example, in the key of A, you might bend an F#, the sixth, up a half tone to the ♭7, or else a tone and a half to the octave. Meanwhile E, the fifth of A, a tone below, might be bent a whole-and-a-half tone up to the ♭7. (See String bend I.)

Minor third bends are a blues-rock staple that feature in String bend II.

Bending only the notes that will reinforce and enhance the feel of the music is the hallmark of the harmonically-aware player and can be developed with practice. You will also find that you develop a feel for bending fretted notes downward from their stretched interval to their normal position from a damped, silent start.

Excepting the high and low E strings, strings may be bent upward or down. For smaller quarter- or half-tone bends, your first finger should be strong enough. For larger bends (such as bending the tonic up to the minor-third one-and-a-half tones above), use your third finger so that you can support it if necessary with the other two—the aim is to avoid the string slipping out from beneath the tip of your finger, producing a noise that no guitarist, or audience for that matter, wants to hear! Using your third finger has the advantage of allowing you to execute a chromatic or whole-tone pull-off once you have released the bend to the normal fretted position.

TRACK 21/1

STRING BEND I

Minor pentatonic licks over a root-chord vamp. Focus on producing accurate bends that are neither sharp nor flat.

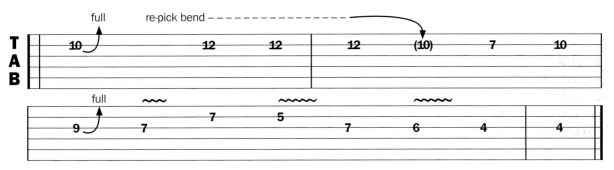

TRACK 21/2

STRING BEND II

There are seven beats to the bar in the following riff. Count each bar of 7/4 as a bar of 4/4 followed by a bar of 3/4. It is reminiscent of one of Pink Floyd's classy riffs. The bend is used sparingly on the minor third.

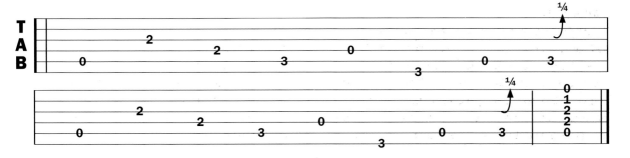

Vibrato

As with string bends and slides, vibrato is a technique that requires firm fingers. The aim is to add color, excitement, and depth to lead lines. Once you are sure of your vibrato techniques, you will be surprised at how plain your playing might sound without it, and you will find yourself using it without thinking, especially on the end note of a solo or phrase.

Vibrato is an oscillation in the note—a slight pitch change usually of around a quarter tone. With practice and development in finger strength, you can master complete control over its rate and depth. The fretted note is moved up and down rather than from side to side, as on a nylon-strung classical guitar.

Gentle vibrato is achieved by moving the fingers most of all, maintaining a radial motion, rotating your wrist in

small, circular movements so that your fingertip moves up and down with a little more momentum than if you were only using your finger strength, and more fluidity than if you were locking your fingers and moving your wrist.

Then again, B.B. King's fast vibrato derives from a whole-hand movement, while Eric Clapton pioneered "freehand" vibrato, in which the only part of the fretting hand touching the guitar is the fingertip!

 **TRACK 22/1**

EXERCISE I
A simple E minor scale run with plenty of space for lingering vibrato.

AVOIDING SLIPPING
Stay within the limits of your finger stretch (which will improve with practice) to avoid the string slipping from beneath your fingers. Light-gauge strings are easiest to bend but can sacrifice a little tone compared to heavier gauges.

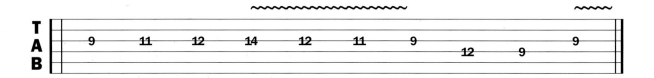

> **I can do the old hand vibrato just fine, but I like attacking the strings.**
>
> *Ritchie Blackmore* (Deep Purple)

Eric Clapton
Master guitarist of
Yardbirds and Cream
fame, to name but
two of his bands,
Clapton's use of
vibrato ranges from
tight twanging to barely
audible. Often he places
a vibrato at the top of
a full tone bend, which
is a great—if tough to
master—way to add
tension to your playing.

TRACK 22/2

EXERCISE II

Try adding vibrato evenly to each note of these arpeggios. You
can extend your vibrato techniques to include diads, triads, and
chords, producing polyphonic vibrato even on a fixed-bridge guitar.

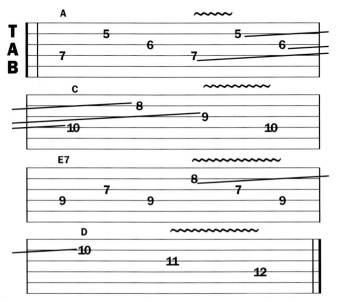

THE VIBRATO BAR

This is the correct name for a tremolo
arm, trem, or tremolo system, nicknames
that derive from Leo Fender's mistaken
use of that term, but which are used so
much they're interchangeable. The effect
produced is vibrato—a change in pitch.
Correctly speaking, tremolo is a change in
volume. Vibrato bars allow the change in
pitch to go down as well as up.

Leaving aside vintage trems such
as the Bigsby, you're most likely to
encounter variations on either the standard
Stratocaster vibrato system, or a Floyd
Rose- or Kahler–style one. The former is
great for smaller oscillations but will have
tuning issues when it comes to metal
styles of "dive-bombing"—extreme string-
detensioning—of which the latter two are
capable without going out of tune.

The Minor Pentatonic
and Minor Blues Scales

The minor pentatonic scale is one of the most important scales in rock music. Being a minor scale, it fits over minor chords perfectly. However, many players also force the scale over major and dominant chords. The minor blues scale adds an extra note to the minor pentatonic: the ♭5. It is this interval that adds that dark, menacing quality that is important in heavy metal riffs (think Black Sabbath or Megadeth), and the extra note makes fast, three-notes-per-string patterns easy.

Here we look at two patterns for both scales: open and movable. Open patterns can be played in only one position; a movable pattern can be played anywhere on the neck, as its name suggests. There are five positions of each scale here.

> "We all have idols. Play like anyone you care about, but try to be yourself while you're doing so."
>
> *B.B. King*

MINOR PENTATONIC SCALE

The first example is the open **E minor** pentatonic scale. It starts on the lowest note of the guitar (open sixth string) and ascends over two octaves to the third fret on the first string. The colored "o's" to the left indicate the open strings to be played.

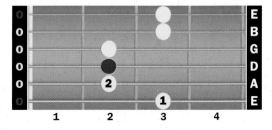

The second example is the **A minor** pentatonic, with the lowest note starting on the fifth fret, sixth string. There are five scale positions (see page 62).

SCALE FORMULA
R–♭3–4–5–♭7–Oct

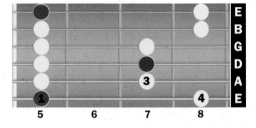

MINOR BLUES SCALE

The minor blues scale is essentially the minor pentatonic with an extra note. The two-octave open pattern adds an extra note on the fifth and third strings. Make sure you use the fingering pattern indicated.

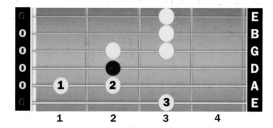

 TRACK 23/4

Here, the **A minor** blues scale pattern is shown with the starting note on the fifth fret of the sixth string. Just like the A minor pentatonic scale, there are five scale positions.

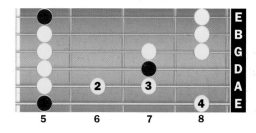

SCALE FORMULA
R–♭3–4–♭5–5–♭7–Oct

B.B. King plays a variation of the blues scale. King has a special vibrato technique: the only part of his left hand that touches the guitar is the finger that does the vibrato.

Minor Pentatonic
Patterns and Licks

There are five scale patterns of the minor pentatonic, just as there are for other scale types. Here are the patterns, with the positions of the tonic (the root notes) indicated. Try running the patterns from any root note you like—or from any note of the scale, as long as you are aware of where the root notes are—and see how quickly you can name the notes you're playing, given that the scale formula is: 1–♭3–4–5–♭7–Octave.

On pages 66 and 67, we'll look at how you can apply these scale patterns imaginatively to any given chord progression in any key. The idea, of course, is not just to run these scales without thinking, just because they'll sound fine! (Although that's great, too.) Scales are just the way we have of "filing" what's in tune and what isn't. Cool licks are to be found in chord fragments and have everything to do with the underlying chord progression, repetition, unisons, bends, phrasing, and "feel"—the subjects covered in this chapter.

Opposite are two exercises that represent just a handful of the ways that interest can be added even to simple minor pentatonic licks, with their underlying chord changes indicated. These include rhythmic (time value) changes, the addition of notes from the blues scale, and the addition of chromatic runs—all achieved with simple picking and the most minimal of bends.

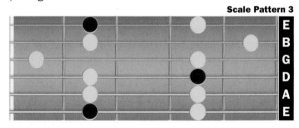

Scale Pattern 3

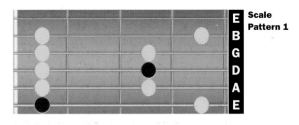

Scale Pattern 1

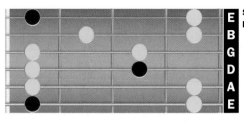

Scale Pattern 4

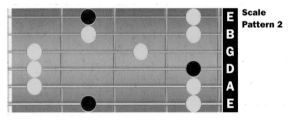

Scale Pattern 2

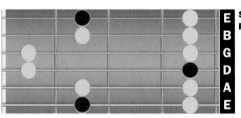

Scale Pattern 5

EXERCISE I

Simple minor pentatonic lick used as a fill in an A5 vamp.

THE INDEX-FINGER "ROLL"

When playing or writing licks, there will be times that you'll want to play notes at the same fret on adjacent strings, one after the other, C on the B string to G on the D string, for example. You would think it a simple matter of making a barre with your first finger. Well, if you do, the notes will ring at once, possibly leading to messy, muddy harmonic activity you don't really want.

For a smooth glissando effect with single notes, make a barre with the top pad of your first finger and roll it, damping the strings you don't want to sound as you fret the one you do. This takes a bit of practice but may prove very useful—especially for sweep picking (see pages 36 and 37).

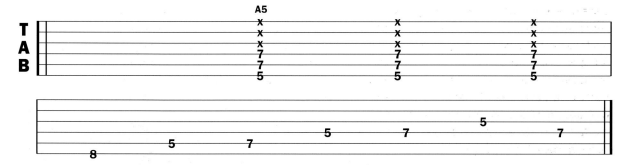

EXERCISE II

Simple minor pentatonic lick used against an E7#9th chord.

"I guess music, particularly the blues, is the only form of schizophrenia that has organized itself into being both legal and beneficial to society."

Alexis Korner, "Father of British Blues," on the power of music

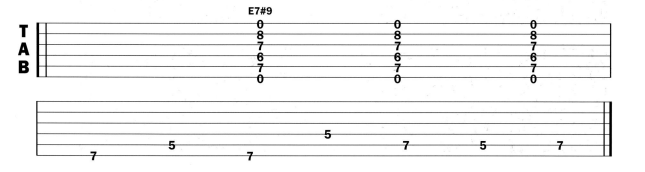

The Major Pentatonic
and Major Blues Scales

The major pentatonic scale is the one from which the minor pentatonic and minor blues scales featured on pages 60 and 61 are derived. Quite simply, it is the five-note scale of any major key, just as the major scale featured on page 22 is the heptatonic, or seven-note, scale. In the key of C, for example, the major pentatonic will consist of C, D, E, G, and A.

The minor pentatonic can be played against the chords from minor keys or forced against major and dominant chords, while the major pentatonic can be played with major chords. Alternating phrases from the minor and major pentatonic scales is one way to develop your understanding of "feel"-based blues guitar soloing.

> **❝Playing scales is like a boxer skipping rope or punching a bag. It's not the thing in itself; it's preparatory to the activity.❞**
>
> **Barney Kessel,** *American jazz guitarist*

 TRACK 25/2

The first example is the open G major pentatonic scale. It ascends over two octaves to the third fret on the first string. The numbers on the red and yellow dots indicate which fingers play the fretted notes.

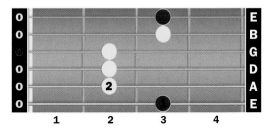

 TRACK 26/1

The second example is the C major pentatonic scale, with the lowest note starting on the eighth fret, sixth string.

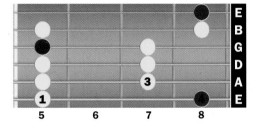

SCALE FORMULA
R–2–3–5–6–Oct

Duane Eddy
One of the earliest guitar heroes, Duane Eddy put the twang—a reverberating, bass-heavy guitar sound—into rock 'n' roll. His unique playing style involved picking single-note melodies on the low strings.

 TRACK 26/2

The major blues scale, shown here in G, is essentially the major pentatonic with an added minor third (♭3). The two-octave pattern adds an extra note on the fifth and third strings.

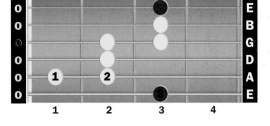

 TRACK 26/3

Here, the C major blues-scale pattern is shown with the starting note on the eighth fret of the sixth string. There are five scale positions for each major, major pentatonic, and major blues scales, just as there are for their relative minors.

SCALE FORMULA
R–2–♭3–3–5–6–Oct

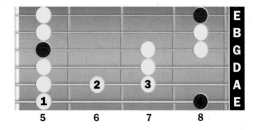

Major Pentatonic
Patterns and Licks

There are five scale patterns of the major pentatonic, just as there are for its minor. These are shown below with the positions of the tonic (root notes) indicated. And as for the pentatonic minor positions, run the patterns from any root note you like—or from any note of the scale, as long as you are aware of where the root notes are—and see how quickly you can name the notes you're playing. The scale formula is: 1–2–3–5–6–Octave.

The application of these scales to chord progressions is covered on pages 68 and 69. The same comments apply here regarding the practical use of scales in your jams, as opposed to how you practice them, that apply to their relative pentatonic minor scales (see pages 60 and 61). Where the minor pentatonic can be played over tonic minor chords, dominant (V), and major chords, the major pentatonic, in addition to being played over major chords, can also be played over dominant seventh chords, since there's no seventh in the scale. Because there is no fourth or seventh, this scale is your one-stop shop for soloing in major keys.

Be aware of the relationship between major scales and their relative minors (see pages 32 and 33). Shape 1 major pentatonic patterns are the same as shape 2 minor pentatonic ones, though the root notes—and the intervals built upon them—differ.

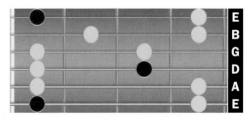

Scale Pattern 3

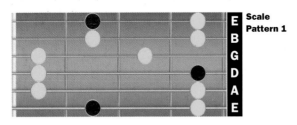

Scale Pattern 1

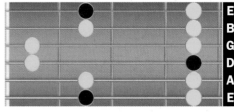

Scale Pattern 4

Scale Pattern 2

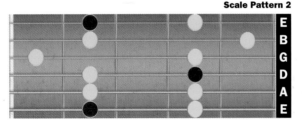

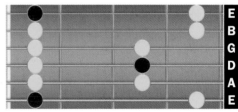

Scale Pattern 5

Stevie Ray Vaughan
A stunningly accomplished guitar player, Stevie Ray Vaughan almost single-handedly brought about the blues revival of the 1980s. Drawing inspiration equally from blues and rock 'n' roll, with a bit of jazz thrown in, Vaughan developed a uniquely eclectic and fiery style of playing.

 **TRACK 26/4**

EXERCISE I

Major pentatonic lick in B.

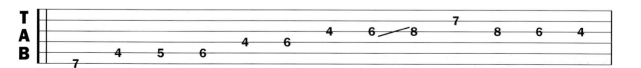

 **TRACK 27/1**

EXERCISE II

Major pentatonic lick in D.

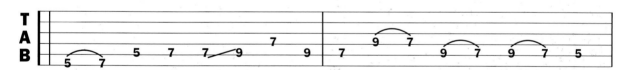

The Secrets of Slick
Solos and Licks

We've discussed how scales are really ways of organizing knowledge as much as something to play. Hitting the notes and finding the intervals that can take people's breath away is every guitarist's holy grail, whether they're into fast-picking country twang or lambent, flowing lead lines. So how do you solo, or find a melody, as good as the ones that made you want to pick up a guitar (a real one, not a game-controller) in the first place?

We can run up and down scales as much as we like, but without knowing how to apply scales to chord progressions, we're all dressed up with nowhere—on the fretboard—to go. Fortunately, there's a procedure for getting started on this that's so straightforward it's almost cheating.

Just to recap, we've seen how major scales relate to their relative minors. In the same way, the major scale is relative to the minor scale, the major pentatonic is relative to the minor pentatonic, and the major blues scale—pentatonic with the addition of its minor third—is the relative major of its minor blues scale. That's not to say that you can only follow each scale type with its corresponding relative—far from it. But it's useful to know how they relate in theory. Going forward, in line with convention, "pentatonic" refers to the major pentatonic, and it'll be qualified as the "minor pentatonic" where this is what is meant.

Here are the five positions of the pentatonic scale:

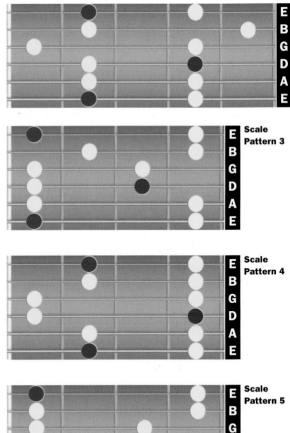

The same root notes apply to the minor pentatonic and blues scales. Let's say we want to solo over this:

D / / / G / / / A / / / D / / /

This is a fairly typical 16-bar progression. Look at the chord chart and you will see that it's in D major.

(Don't worry if the progression is more complex. In conjunction with listening to what sounds right and wrong, you will soon develop an ability to hear and determine the tonal center, based on the most crucial chords—progressions may also contain chords from outside the key, which needn't be confusing. The tonal center is derived from the majority of the chords.)

Pattern 1 will work on D (10th fret, low E); Pattern 2 will work on E (12th fret); Pattern 3 on F# (2nd fret); Pattern 4 on A (5th fret) and Pattern 5 on B (7th fret)—the notes of D pentatonic.

Choose a scale pattern (the one you like most, or want to use—this is art, after all, and choice is involved!). Looking at the chart, follow the column up from your chosen pattern number until it intersects with the key your song or chord sequence is in. Play the pattern so that it begins on the root of the chord where it intersects the key.

So, for our progression above, let's say you like the sound of Pattern 5. You would begin this pattern on B.

Key Chord Chart

I	II	III	IV	V	VI	VII
C	Dm	Em	F	G	Am	B°
D♭	E♭m	Fm	G♭	A♭	B♭m	C°
D	Em	F#m	G	A	Bm	C#°
E♭	Fm	Gm	A♭	B♭	Cm	D°
E	F#m	G#m	A	B	C#m	D#°
F	Gm	Am	B♭	C	Dm	E°
F#	G#m	A#m	B	C#	D#m	E#°
G	Am	Bm	C	D	Em	F#°
A♭	B♭m	Cm	D♭	E♭	Fm	G°
A	Bm	C#m	D	E	F#m	G#°
B♭	Cm	Dm	E♭	F	Gm	A°
B	C#m	D#m	E	F#	G#m	A#°
Scale Pattern 1	Scale Pattern 2	Scale Pattern 3		Scale Pattern 4	Scale Pattern 5	

Spotlight on
Modality

Once you have jammed a few times with the method on the previous pages, you will realize that it equips you with a key to access just about all of the great major- and minor-scale blues and rock licks you can shake your axe at! Great blues careers have been built on less.

They are also responsible for most of the sounds you will hear in classic rock, and even metal (see pages 116 and 117 for some other great scales). You could spend a lifetime exploring them and not exhaust the possibilities, which is true for just about any single way of looking at music. Take Slash, for example: "I don't use a lot of weird tunings because I'm still trying to accomplish playing the guitar the way it is."

A mode is created with either its scale pattern or its tonic chord. Modal thinking opens up yet another way of approaching the fretboard. You can analyze an existing progression in modal terms for ideas to play against

it, or use your insight to suggest new parts for a song you're writing. The humble major scale (see pages 22 and 23) is the basis for the modes that are most often heard in rock. Mixolydian choruses are likely to be strong and memorable, for example, following an Ionian verse progression.

The major scale can be made to evoke seven different musical moods, depending on which note of the scale is emphasized as the tonic note. A mode is not a new scale type built on that note but a continuation of the intervals of the major scale, starting at that note and ending an octave higher. Modes match the intervals in a chord progression (where it doesn't change key). For example, B♭, the dominant seventh of F, (I), crops up in the Mixolydian mode and is also often added to the C chord (V) as the dominant seventh—two different ways of thinking, producing the same harmonic result. You can hear from the triads (the first three notes—see pages 22 and 23) of each mode whether its corresponding chord will be major or minor, and vice versa.

Modal patterns are not an infallible guide to staying on the harmonic straight and narrow, so keep listening out for any new keys you may have modulated into. However, they are a great way to think of lead lines and chord progressions—and get around the neck, whether you're composing or looking to bring imaginative lead parts to an existing progression.

Joe Satriani
Without a doubt, Satch is of the most technically accomplished and widely respected guitarists of recent times and—unsurprisingly—has taught many of the best contemporary rock guitarists the secrets of great playing.

Mode Scale Patterns
and their Moods

We will indicate contrasting modal sounds in each of the songs at the end of the following chapters.

TRACKS 27/2—29

Ionian—Regular Major
TRACK 27/2

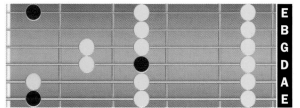

Root Interval = Tonic
Associated Chord = Major

Dorian—Jazzy
TRACK 27/3

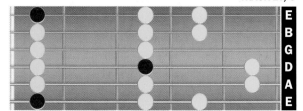

Root Interval = 2nd
Associated Chord = Minor

Phrygian—Flamenco
TRACK 27/4

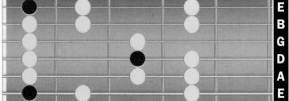

Root Interval = 3rd
Associated Chord = Minor

Lydian—Jazzy
TRACK 27/4

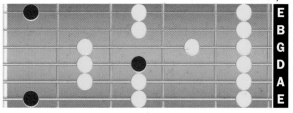

Root Interval = 4th (Sub-Dominant)
Associated Chord = Major

Mixolydian—Rock
TRACK 28/1

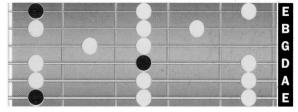

Root Interval = 5th (Dominant)
Associated Chord = Major

Aeolian—Relative Minor
TRACK 28/2

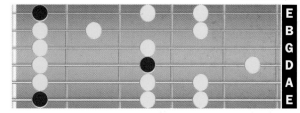

Root Interval = 6th
Associated Chord = Minor

Locrian—Tense, Unresolved
TRACK 29

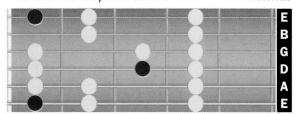

Root Interval = 7th
Associated Chord = Diminished

Play the Blues

Many of the great blues legends' lives were short and shrouded in folklore and mystery. Robert Johnson, the original Delta blues pioneer, was said to have traded his soul to the devil in exchange for his incredible musical talent. Then there's the song content itself, often telling a woeful tale of cheating lovers or the bullying big boss man.

But, for our purposes, what is the blues in musical terms? First, there were work songs, motivational chants with a question-and-answer feel. Much music with a blues feel still retains exactly this—but it is the lead guitar that will often "answer" a singer's question or statement with a blistering, expressive lick in the two or four bars that follow. "Blue notes" are commonly flattened thirds (the minor third), fifths, and sevenths.

They occur not only in the blues but in Irish and English traditional music too. In the following chapter, we will work toward building complete sections of blues-style music, applying the minor pentatonic and minor blues scales learned in the previous chapter. You will see how the use of these scales over pieces of music in a major key produces the unique harmonic feel of the blues.

Gibson 335
The Gibson ES-335 is the world's first commercial thinline, arched-top, semi-acoustic electric guitar. Favored by Foo Fighters's Dave Grohl and Blink-182's Tom DeLonge, the 335 is neither hollow nor solid; instead, a solid wood block runs through the center of its body.

Twelve-Bar Blues
Progressions

The twelve-bar blues chord progression has stood the tests of time and taste thanks to its simplicity. It's a durable concept that has survived its incorporation into successive genres so that, like the blues scale, its name is deceptive in that it does not occur only in the blues but in jazz, funk, rock, and heavy rock styles too. Many universally famous pop hits such as "Johnny B. Goode," "Blue Suede Shoes," "Rock around the Clock," and "Shake, Rattle and Roll" are straightforward examples.

The twelve-bar consists of the I (tonic), IV (subdominant), and V (dominant) chords in any key, played in a repeated "turnaround" pattern, i.e. one which leads the ear back to the tonic chord.

Each line consists of sixteen quarter notes. Here's how the twelve bars break down in their most basic form, tabled into groups of four simply to make it easier to remember:

I – I – I – I
IV – IV – I – I
V – VI – I – I

Generally, when we substitute something we swap one thing for another, but in music, "chord substitution" refers not only to swapping chords for others but also to the harmonic alterations possible within those chords themselves. The twelve-bar is ripe for both kinds of substitution.

The altered chords that you will hear most commonly in a twelve-bar with a blues or rock feel will be sevenths and ninths, explained on pages 68 and 69. There are

"Hearing the blues changed my life."

Van Morrison

TRACK 30

EXERCISE I
The bare bones of a twelve-bar blues progression, in E.

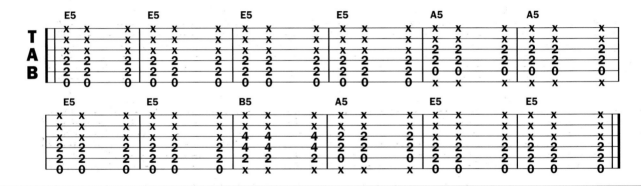

many possible chord substitutions within the twelve-bar. And bear in mind that there are also eight-, sixteen-, and thirty-two-bar blues too.

For all three exercises, experiment with strumming the given chord voicings with solid, rhythmic up and down strokes; with downstrokes only; with damping, and without. Syncopate, or accent by means of damping, the beats of the bar that feel most natural to you, as well as the offbeats (the pulses for which you count "and"). You should find yourself achieving this partly with your fretting hand by releasing your fingers from the frets but not losing contact with the strings. If you don't, it's something to practice.

Experiment with damping the second and fourth beats together, then the first and third. The first should produce a rockier feel than the second.

 TRACK 31

EXERCISE II

A twelve-bar in A. Note the sense of anticipation that comes from accenting the second and fourth beats.

 TRACK 32

EXERCISE III

Ending the twelve-bar cycle on the dominant (V) is known as a "turnaround," which leads naturally to the tonic.

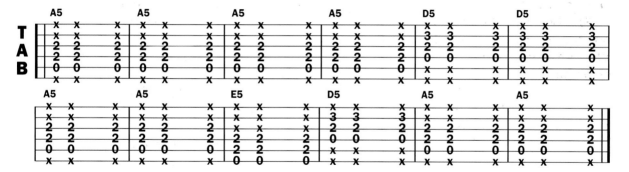

Open-Chord Blues
Progressions

If you plan to jam with your guitar-playing buddies or audition for a band, chances are someone will suggest starting off with a twelve-bar. It's almost a "social grace" for rock musicians, like playing parlor songs was for young Victorian women. Be sure to have the manners to trade rhythm and lead parts, and let someone else solo once in a while.

The blues involves a different way of thinking from compositional song structure. The common progressions provide a "test bed" on which to learn those licks, bends, and other harmonic elements that will and won't work. Think of blues lead styles, like vocal, as holding a conversation. Aim to hold the listener's interest just as you do when you speak. Alternate "shouts" and "whispers," and aim to play on and around the beat.

Your goal is to add interest to a tried and tested formula, as opposed to playing music that derives its interest from original harmonic compositional content, like a pop song. Then you'll be in a position to add blues-inspired elements to your songs.

Shuffle licks: The most common way to add interest to the simple rhythm part of the twelve-bar blues' I–IV–V–I progression is to add shuffle licks. The shuffle lick drew its inspiration from the rhythmic left-hand vamping of boogie-woogie piano players. It similarly involves playing alternating phrases, typically between the two notes of a diad or the three notes of a triad, along with notes of the chords to keep the key signature emphasized.

Extra notes from within the scale of the chord are added on the offbeats: Exercise I adds a sixth to the power-chord structures from pages 44 and 45 while Exercise II adds the minor seventh as well as the sixth. You will hear how these add harmonic color and syncopation without changing the essential turnaround feel that leads the listener back to the tonic chord, with its sense of resolution. These utilize root-note open strings,

TRACK 33

EXERCISE I

As with all exercises, begin slowly and speed up your metronome incrementally as you learn. Exercises I and II lend themselves well to damping with your strumming hand. Notice as you increase the tempo that the character changes from a laid-back boogie in the manner of J.J. Cale to an urgency that helps to emphasize the driving, bluesy minor seventh.

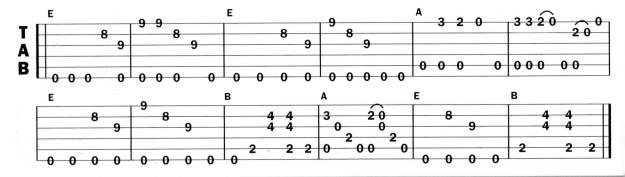

while Exercise III demonstrates how the same intervals can be placed within fifth chord structures similar to the open chords featured on pages 24 and 25, but with the thirds removed, utilizing the open strings for notes other than the root and introducing a more jangly feel.

The previous exercises, on pages 74 and 75, were designed to teach the twelve-bar structure and some of its possible substitutions, and were lacking the rhythmic content provided by shuffle licks. Why not try adding shuffle licks to those as well?

Bruce Springsteen
Heartland rock infused with blues, folk, and rock 'n' roll makes Springsteen's intense ballads and rousing anthems so popular.

 TRACK 34

EXERCISE II

```
     A5          A5          A5          A5          D5          D5
   x  x  x  x   x  x  x  x   x  x  x  x   x  x  x  x   x  x  x  x   x  x  x  x
T  x  x  x  x   x  x  x  x   x  x  x  x   x  x  x  x   3  3  3  3   3  3  3  3
A  2  2  2  2   2  2  2  2   2  2  2  2   2  2  2  2   2  4  2  4   2  4  2  4
B  2  4  2  4   2  2  2  2   2  4  2  4   2  4  2  4   0  0  0  0   0  0  0  0
   0  0  0  0   0  0  0  0   0  0  0  0   0  0  0  0   x  x  x  x   x  x  x  x
   x  x  x  x   x  x  x  x   x  x  x  x   x  x  x  x   x  x  x  x   x  x  x  x

     A5          A5          E5          D5          A5          A5
   x  x  x  x   x  x  x  x   x  x  x  x   x  x  x  x   x  x  x  x   x  x  x  x
   x  x  x  x   x  x  x  x   x  x  x  x   3  3  3  3   x  x  x  x   x  x  x  x
   2  2  2  2   2  2  2  2   x  x  x  x   2  4  2  4   2  2  2  2   2  2  2  2
   2  4  2  4   2  4  2  4   2  2  2  2   0  0  0  0   2  4  2  4   2  4  2  4
   0  0  0  0   0  0  0  0   2  4  2  4   x  x  x  x   0  0  0  0   0  0  0  0
   x  x  x  x   x  x  x  x   0  0  0  0   x  x  x  x   x  x  x  x   x  x  x  x
```

 TRACK 35

EXERCISE III

Strum Exercise III firmly and evenly with up and down strokes. This should produce a rhythm part that would be at home in a Tom Petty or Bruce Springsteen song.

```
     E5          E5          E5          E5          A5          A5
   x  x  x  x   x  x  x  x   x  x  x  x   x  x  x  x   x  x  x  x   x  x  x  x
T  x  x  x  x   x  x  x  x   x  x  x  x   x  x  x  x   x  x  x  x   x  x  x  x
A  x  x  x  x   x  x  x  x   x  x  x  x   x  x  x  x   2  2  2  2   2  2  2  2
B  2  2  2  2   2  2  2  2   2  2  2  2   2  2  2  2   2  4  5  4   2  4  5  4
   2  4  5  4   2  4  5  4   2  4  5  4   2  4  5  4   0  0  0  0   0  0  0  0
   0  0  0  0   0  0  0  0   0  0  0  0   0  0  0  0   x  x  x  x   x  x  x  x

     E5          E5          B5          A5          E5          E5
   x  x  x  x   x  x  x  x   x  x  x  x   x  x  x  x   x  x  x  x   x  x  x  x
   x  x  x  x   x  x  x  x   x  x  x  x   x  x  x  x   x  x  x  x   x  x  x  x
   x  x  x  x   x  x  x  x   x  x  x  x   2  2  2  2   x  x  x  x   x  x  x  x
   2  2  2  2   2  2  2  2   9  9  9  9   2  4  5  4   2  2  2  2   2  2  2  2
   2  4  5  4   2  4  5  4   9  11 12 11  0  0  0  0   2  4  5  4   2  4  5  4
   0  0  0  0   0  0  0  0   7  7  7  7   x  x  x  x   0  0  0  0   0  0  0  0
```

Barre-Chord Blues
Progressions

By now it'll be apparent that I–IV–V–I progressions form a boxlike shape visually in standard tuning. This can be applied to any area of the neck. Of course, thinking this way will only get you so far, and it's important to retain your musical insight in the intervals you use, wherever you're playing on the neck.

While the majority of blues-rock pieces you'll encounter will be played in the guitar-friendly keys of C, A, G, E, D, this knowledge is especially useful for popular jazz keys, such as B♭, which suit keyboards and brass and for that reason occur in funk and soul music too. As your intervallic thinking grows, chances are you'll also originate your own movable shapes. In the meantime, typical examples with alternative whole-chord substitutions appear in Exercises I and II.

If you're not a fan of the twelve-bar blues it's possible that you've only heard examples that haven't appealed to you. There are many gripping pieces of music built around a simple twelve-bar structure, but not obviously so,

since they avoid idioms such as shuffle licks (see pages 76 and 77) and dominant sevenths, dominant because they are being used to lead the ear to the tonic, unlike a major seventh, which feels more static and sounds more mellifluous—see pages 178 and 179).

Exercise III features a jazz-inspired twelve-bar to illustrate this point and also show how movable blues progressions lend themselves well to altered chords featuring less common intervals than fifths, sixths, and minor sevenths, such as ninths.

Blues in minor keys can be especially driving and forceful, and many well-known blues songs have featured the I–IV–V–I progression played in a minor key.

 TRACK 36

EXERCISE I

Twelve-bar in A—the familiar, warm sound of sevenths.

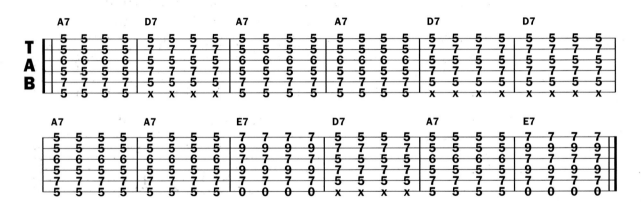

EXERCISE II

The jazzy sound of ninths, in G. Note the D♭ passing chord, which has a short enough value not to sound odd.

```
      G9          C9            G9
   T  10    10    x x x x x x   10       10
   A  10    10    x x x x x x   10       10
      10    10    7 7 7 7 7 7   10       10
   B  9     9     8 8 8 8 8 8   9        9
      10    10    7 7 7 7 7 7   10       10
      x     x     8 8 8 8 8 8   x        x

      G9          C9            C9
      10    10    x x x x x x   x x x x x x
      10    10    x x x x x x   x x x x x x
      10    10    7 7 7 7 7 7   7 7 7 7 7 7
      9     9     8 8 8 8 8 8   8 8 8 8 8 8
      10    10    7 7 7 7 7 7   7 7 7 7 7 7
      x     x     8 8 8 8 8 8   8 8 8 8 8 8

      G9          G9            D9          D♭9
      10    10    10    10      x x x x     x x x x
      10    10    10    10      x x x x     x x x x
      10    10    10    10      9 9 9 9     8
      9     9     9     9       10 10 10 10 9
      10    10    10    10      9 9 9 9     8
      x     x     x     x       10 10 10 10 9

      C9          G9            D9
      x x x x x x 10    10      x x x x x x
      x x x x x x 10    10      x x x x x x
      7 7 7 7 7 7 10    10      9 9 9 9 9 9
      8 8 8 8 8 8 9     9       10 10 10 10 10 10
      7 7 7 7 7 7 10    10      9 9 9 9 9 9
      8 8 8 8 8 8 x     x       10 10 10 10 10 10
```

Billy Gibbons
Power trio ZZ Top's guitarist Billy Gibbons's exceptional guitar playing and muscular riffs make him unquestionably one of the finest blues-rock guitarists of modern times.

TRACK 38

EXERCISE III

Sharp ninths and thirteenths are reminiscent of soul and Stax twelve-bars. Stax Records was a record label in Memphis, Tennessee that was a major influence in the creation of Southern soul, early funk, and 1960's Chicago blues.

```
      E7#9        A13           E7#9          E7#9          A13           A13
   T  0     0     x x x x x x   0 0 0 0 0 0   0 0 0 0 0 0   x x x x x x   x x x x x x
   A  8     8     7 7 7 7 7 7   8 8 8 8 8 8   8 8 8 8 8 8   7 7 7 7 7 7   7 7 7 7 7 7
      7     7     6 6 6 6 6 6   7 7 7 7 7 7   7 7 7 7 7 7   6 6 6 6 6 6   6 6 6 6 6 6
   B  7     7     5 5 5 5 5 5   6 6 6 6 6 6   6 6 6 6 6 6   5 5 5 5 5 5   5 5 5 5 5 5
      7     7     x x x x x x   7 7 7 7 7 7   7 7 7 7 7 7   x x x x x x   x x x x x x
      0 0   0 0   5 5 5 5 5 5   0 0 0 0 0 0   0 0 0 0 0 0   5 5 5 5 5 5   5 5 5 5 5 5

      E7#9          E7#9          B13       A13         A13#5   E7#9          B13
      0 0 0 0 0 0   0 0 0 0 0 0   x x       x x x x     x x x x 0 0 0 0 0 0   x x
      8 8 8 8 8 8   8 8 8 8 8 8   9 9       7 7 7 7     7 7 7 7 8 8 8 8 8 8   9 9
      7 7 7 7 7 7   7 7 7 7 7 7   8 8       6 6 6 6     6 6 6 6 7 7 7 7 7 7   8 8
      6 6 6 6 6 6   6 6 6 6 6 6   7 7       5 5 5 5     5 5 5 5 6 6 6 6 6 6   7 7
      7 7 7 7 7 7   7 7 7 7 7 7   x x       x x x x     x x x x 7 7 7 7 7 7   x x
      0 0 0 0 0 0   0 0 0 0 0 0   7 7       x x x x     5 5 5 5 0 0 0 0 0 0   7 7
```

Open and Easy
Blues Licks

These exercises feature blues licks in E and use the minor pentatonic. They're typical of licks that fit a common twelve-bar progression, and should give an insight into just how easy it is to create simple phrases that can move effectively against the I, IV, and V of any key.

This way of thinking will help you to locate starting points for phrases or solos at any fret: why not find all the positions in which you can play these phrases, even those above the twelfth fret? (Remembering that the twelfth fret is the octave for each string will help you to move away from the comfort zone provided by the lower frets.)

If you know which interval your opening note represents within the key in which you are playing (B as the fifth of E, for example), then you can work out the note that represents the corresponding interval for any other key (by playing and counting a major or minor scale on your fretboard from its tonic, if necessary). Armed with this knowledge, you can work toward mapping on your fretboard the neck positions in which you can play a phrase such as those below in any given key and, for your favorite phrases, the fret at which you would begin them if playing within the other popular keys for the guitar.

The rest of the chapter looks at how you might begin to come up with those licks themselves, based on some firm favorites from the history of the blues.

TRACK 39/1

EXERCISE I

Unison bends, in which a lower note is bent a whole tone up, sounding in unison with a higher note on an adjacent string, are a defining feature of blues-rock solos.

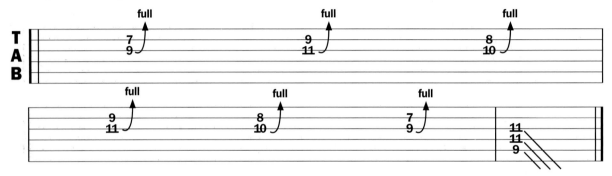

Jeff Beck

Innovative, tasteful, and visionary, Jeff Beck has been called "one of the most influential lead guitarists in rock." One of the three noted guitarists to have played with The Yardbirds—along with Eric Clapton and Jimmy Page—much of Beck's recorded music has been instrumental, with a focus on innovative sound and spanning genres ranging from blues-rock, heavy metal, jazz fusion, and a blend of guitar-rock and electronica. He was ranked No. 14 in *Rolling Stone* magazine's "100 Greatest Guitarists of All Time."

> ❝ **I don't care about the rules. In fact, if I don't break the rules at least ten times in every song then I'm not doing my job properly.** ❞
>
> *Jeff Beck*

TRACK 39/2

EXERCISE II

Bluesy slides against open strings are easy in E and A. This one uses notes from the E minor pentatonic scale.

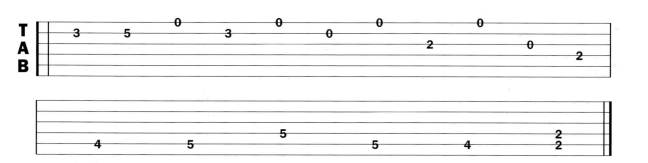

Writing Your Own
Blues Licks

The art of great blues licks and solos depends as much on listening to the band, or your jam track, and giving some thought to what's going to be most effective, as it does on fast, flash fingerings. Sure, it can feel great to execute a fast run in your soloing, but that's something to master once you have an insight into how the melodies you are playing sound against the harmony parts.

Don't forget that scales are only a means of organizing information—don't think for a minute that you have to play their notes in a series. Think of ways to break them up, create unexpected intervals, and experiment with phrasing: playing before, on, or after the beat can put the emphasis on different notes, radically changing the ways that very similar phrases feel.

These exercises feature simple phrases in A. They both consist of only five notes (and their octaves). When played against the given chords or root notes, they should introduce an effective blues feel that's familiar from many

EXTENDED CHORDS
Extended chords can look confusing, whether you're coming up with a progression or with licks to play against one. It helps to know that they're often an octave above a more familiar interval and function similarly. For example:

2nd ——————— 9th
4th ——————— 11th
6th ——————— 13th

TRACK 40/1

EXERCISE I
Listen for the way in which the chords move beneath the solo. Exercise I features the tonic.

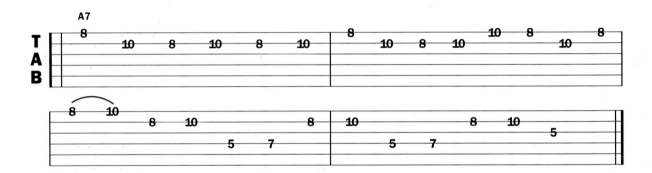

Mike Bloomfield

classic tracks. This is because they are major over the I chord, and minor over the IV and V chords, creating tension and drive.

This is achieved because a half-tone bend on the eighth fret of the top E string will take you from C, the minor third of A, to C#, the major third. They form a simple, boxlike shape (consisting of G—the minor seventh, A—the tonic, C, C#, and D—the fifth), but nonetheless, when it comes to the theory, they combine two scale types—the major and minor pentatonic.

Mike Bloomfield
Respected for his fluid guitar playing, Bloomfield, who knew and played with many of Chicago's blues legends even before he achieved his own fame, became one of the first popular music superstars of the 1960s to earn his place entirely on his playing prowess. One of America's first great white blues guitarists, Bloomfield's expressive solo lines and awesome technique also graced most of Bob Dylan's early electric experiments.

 TRACK 40/2

EXERCISE II

This features a sub-dominant and dominant progression resolving to the tonic. It is the chords that create tension and resolution behind the solo.

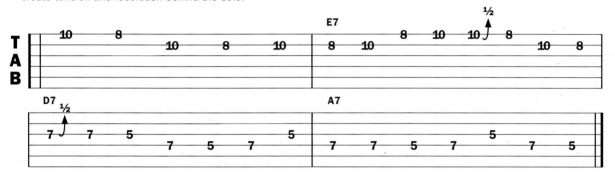

Play Your First
Solo

The following solo expands on the principles explained on pages 82 and 83. Play along with this and you will see how surprisingly easy it is to construct a functional blues solo from just a few notes from within the major and minor pentatonic scales.

This exercise will get you soloing in no time. What distinguishes an expressive solo from simply running the correct scales for a chord sequence according to the patterns on pages 62 and 66 is the player's ability to listen out for the chord sequence against which they are playing, anticipating where the progression is going as they do. Absorb the principle that a solo can be built from the notes that are shared between the major and minor pentatonic and blues scales and you will have gone a

long way toward unlocking the mysterious musical box of tricks that the most authentic players know. Other notes, bends, slides, and runs can then be incorporated according to the individual chord against which they sound effective.

The following solo in A uses only the tonic, the minor third (with whole-tone bends to the major third), the fifth, and the minor seventh (and, for a little variety, their octaves).

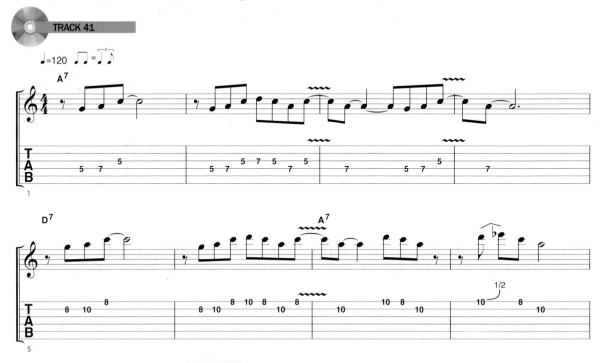

Your First
Blues Song

A solid grounding in the twelve-bar blues will help your understanding of the guitar even if your interest lies in constructing melodic pop from original chord sequences. While it may only consist of I–IV–V progressions in one order or another, it will anchor your sense of harmony around the strongest chords of any scale.

Blues-inspired licks and tricks define the sound of the electric guitar. As a guitarist, you can bring them into just about any other style of music. The following song is inspired by Chicago-style (electric) blues, and the feel of players such as John Lee Hooker. As it progresses, you will hear just how easy it can be to throw in open licks from the (position 1) minor pentatonic scale. These punctuate the basic riff while allowing your fingers enough time to return to it.

TRACK 42

VERSE

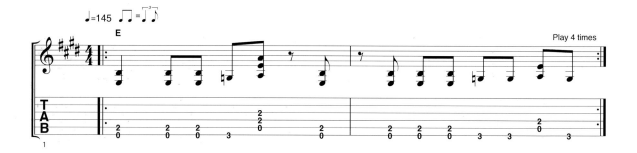

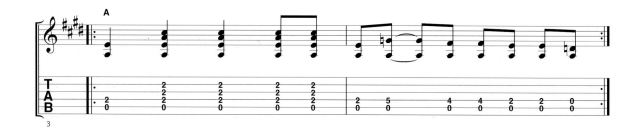

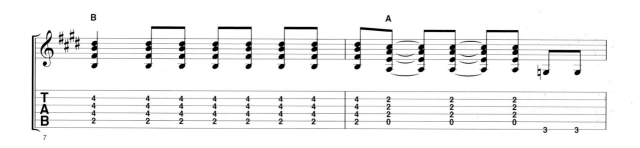

CHORUS

BREAK

Play Rock 'n' Roll

It's widely said that the legendary Ohio DJ Alan Freed coined the phrase "rock 'n' roll." Whether he did or not, he was certainly the "father" of rock 'n' roll. His radio show brought the intoxicating sound of black rhythm & blues music to hungry white teenage audiences across America. Rock 'n' roll pioneers such as Little Richard or Chuck Berry would certainly not have enjoyed their hugely successful careers without him.

In earlier rock 'n' roll hits, piano and saxophone took the lead, but these were squeezed out by the electric guitar by the mid-1950s. The electric bass was also invented by Leo Fender partway through this process, and gone was the characteristic slap of a double bass played without a bow for all but jazz musicians and rockabilly revivalists. Rock 'n' roll is basically a boogie-woogie rhythm with a strong backbeat, usually from the snare drum most of all. Music that had been initially created for self-entertainment was packaged to meet the needs of the new teenage market, and the rock 'n' roll explosion produced clipped, concise lead lines, techniques, and tricks that have not been bettered since.

Gretsch White Falcon
Best known for its large size and distinctive appearance—gleaming white with gold trim—the Gretsch White Falcon, with its handsome look, has always been a much sought-after guitar.

Rock 'n' Roll
Chord Progressions

Most rock 'n' roll hits that remain popular today are based on the twelve-bar blues (see pages 74 and 75). However, the guitarists who played on them had often honed their craft in swing, jazz, or country ensembles, and so incorporated harmonic aspects from these forms.

One of these is the augmented chord: in rock 'n' roll, it is often substituted for the dominant, since it similarly drives the harmony toward the tonic. Augmented chords sound like a complex idea, but you will not go far wrong if you think of them in partnership with diminished chords. We've seen how the third note of a triad determines whether its key is major or minor. While fifths are different from thirds in that there is a perfect fifth (whereas there is no such thing as a third that is neither major nor minor), a major triad with a sharpened fifth is called "augmented,"

while a minor triad with a flattened fifth is called "diminished." Augmented chords are given as "#5," such as "E#5," while diminished chords are conventionally referred to with the following symbol: "°" as in "B°" (since "♭5" would create ambiguity between the root note and the chord type, as in "B♭5").

Exercise I contains a traditional, ringing rock 'n' roll voicing of an augmented chord. Note its role as an introductory chord and as a substitute for the dominant chord in the subsequent twelve-bar progression.

The Beatles
It is not possible to overstate the impact of the Beatles. Even the London *Sunday Times* ballet critic, Richard Buckle, praised them as "the greatest composers since Beethoven." With its crisp harmonies, solid musicianship, and energetic pop instincts, the Beatles's music ignited the energy of youth across the world. Judged on sales and airplay alone, the Beatles are by far the top group in rock 'n' roll history—but their musical legacy had an impact that can still be felt today.

Meanwhile, narrative rock 'n' roll era ballads or
Buddy Holly love songs often use a I–IV–V progression
for verse or chorus, alternated.

 **TRACK 43**

EXERCISE I

A simple rock 'n' roll ballad-style progression in D that leads from verse chords into a potential chorus.

 **TRACK 44**

EXERCISE II

In B♭, a popular rock 'n' roll key used by Chuck Berry among others. The V chord is augmented.

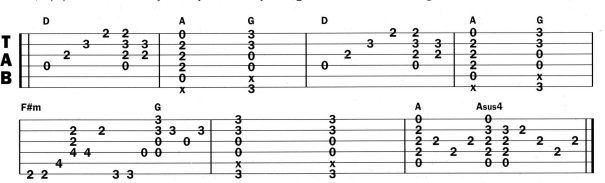

Easy Rock 'n' Roll Licks

Rock 'n' roll draws on elements of country music as well as the blues, and this is reflected in its sparse lead lines and spare, effective solos. These often feature arpeggios, picking a melody out of the notes of the chords, and country-style slides against open strings. These evoke the sound of a lap-steel guitar but are often used to play dissonant grace notes (those too short to have a time value), a half-tone away from a ringing open string, such as the one that begins the first exercise below, which uses the E blues scale (with grace notes) over an E (I) chord.

This lick functions best as a self-contained phrase, or as a song or solo ending, also to be played over the tonic chord. It too features notes fretted against open strings—which sound great when played with ringing, clean tones. It suits the slower, balladic "doo-wop" style that was as much a part of the popular rock 'n' roll scene as uptempo hits with arpeggiated bass lines, and shows a blues influence in its use of the blues scale (see page 64). The pull-offs in the second and third bars require some finger strength. Pull downward and slightly sideways.

The second lick is also shown here in E and is another to play over the tonic chord. The fact that it resolves to the tonic makes it a great all-purpose lick in E major.

> "Rock 'n' roll: music for the neck downward."
>
> **Keith Richards** (The Rolling Stones)

 **TRACK 45/1**

EXERCISE I
A pull-off lick that features the minor third and major sixth against the tonic chord.

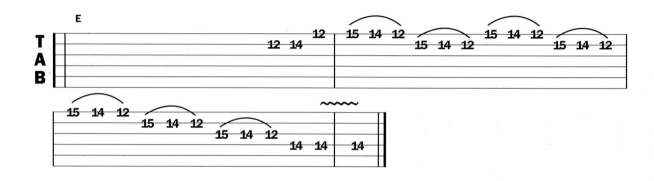

Eddie Cochran

Only twenty-one when he died, Eddie Cochran nevertheless left a contribution to music as a pioneer of rock 'n' roll. With such classics as "C'mon Everybody," "Something Else," and "Summertime Blues," Cochran captured the essence of teenage angst and desire. In his stage presence and performance, Cochran epitomized the look and sound of the rebel rocker.

Rock's First Guitar Hero
A virtuoso guitarist, Cochran played with such authority that music journalist Bruce Eder pronounced him "rock's first high-energy guitar hero, the forerunner to Pete Townshend, Jimmy Page, Duane Allman and, at least in terms of dexterity, Jimi Hendrix."

 **TRACK 45/2**

EXERCISE II

An E-major arpeggio lick that features open strings and chromatic (semitonal) intervals.

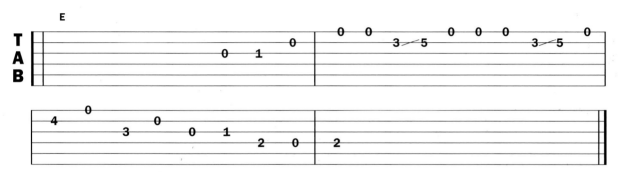

Simple, Movable
Rock 'n' Roll Licks

Remember that rock 'n' roll guitarists such as Franny Beecher, one of Bill Haley's Comets, didn't have distortion tones available to them. However, thanks to the build quality of early valve amps, they had access to bell-like clean tones that have never been bettered.

Driving double stops, such as those in the first exercise below, are a common feature of rock 'n' roll (see pages 98 and 99). Illustrated, once again, in E major, this movable phrase is ideal for transposition. It uses the mixolydian mode (see page 71) but throws in the minor third for a bluesy twist, especially where it occurs in unison with the major sixth in the first bar.

Double-stop phrases like this often lend themselves to arpeggiated picking, as does the phrase featured in the second exercise. Classic rock 'n' roll hits often begin with a single guitar phrase that establishes the tonal center, either with the tonic, or by using the dominant into the tonic. This jaunty example is in B♭ and shows clearly how grace-note chromatic (semitonal) slides can breathe dynamism into the notes of the tonic chord.

The following exercise also uses a "straight eighths" pattern that's typical of the way that double-stop phrases are picked in rock 'n' roll, but is slightly

 **TRACK 46/1**

EXERCISE I

An E-major arpeggio-based double-stop lick (with a minor third in the last bar) where the picking feel changes. This works well over major or dominant seventh chords.

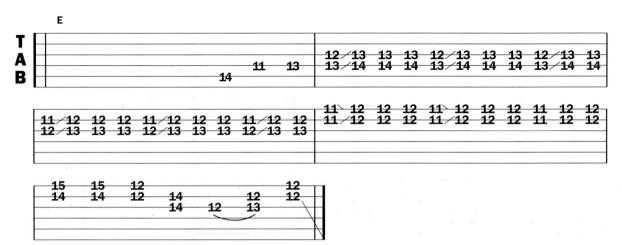

Bill Haley

Hailed as "the father of rock 'n' roll" and "rock 'n' roll's first star," Bill Haley brought rock 'n' roll music into the mainstream. In 1954 Bill Haley and His Comets's anthem "Rock Around the Clock" entered the charts, stayed at No. 1 for eight weeks, and sold twenty-five million copies worldwide. As he told *Rolling Stone* magazine in 1967, "We put country and western together with rhythm and blues, and that was rock." Haley also believed that he had given rock 'n' roll its name—his "Rock-A-Beatin' Boogie" had a chorus that went "Rock, rock, rock everybody, Roll, roll, roll everybody." And, indeed, everybody did.

more harmonically complex since it alternates between the I and IV chords, showing how these figures can be used over a simple progression. It's given in A major, so D is the subdominant chord. Since C is the minor seventh of this chord, its appearance in the lick (forming a flattened fifth with F#, the major third) adds tension.

> **"Rock 'n' roll is good for the soul, for the well being, for the psyche, for your everything. I love it. I can't even picture being without rock 'n' roll."**
>
> *Hank Ballard, rhythm and blues singer and one of the first 1950's proto-rock 'n' roll artists*

 **TRACK 46/2**

EXERCISE II

Played here over IV and I chords, this lick is equally playable over the tonic. The F# and C in the third bar form a flattered fifth, but are derived from the A and D chords.

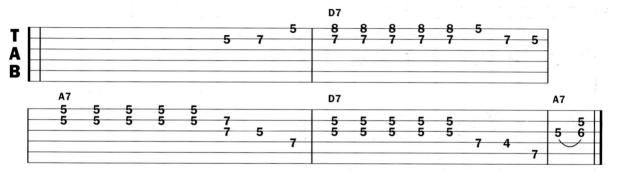

Double-Stop Rock 'n' Roll
Licks and Picking
Techniques

In addition to the licks on the preceding pages, many classic rock 'n' roll licks betray a country flavor as well as being influenced by the blues. In many of these licks, the notes played in the double-stop are not situated on adjacent strings, and so, in keeping with a country twist, some measure of picking, with a finger other than your thumb and index finger, will be required.

These exercises will not require more than one such "extra" finger. In keeping with the scope of the book, they are designed to be played with a pick, together with the pad of your third finger. They're inspired by the rockabilly era of the mid-late 1950s, by which time the electric guitar had established itself as the lead instrument besides the voice. The development of today's lead techniques—appropriated from country licks and slide playing—was just beginning. So focus on your strumming hand until it is finger-pickin' good!

PICKING TECHNIQUES
The most common plectrum-free picking technique is sometimes referred to as "clawhammer" style, popularized by country players such as Merle Travis, in which the side of the thumb is alternated with your fingers. If you can master the coordination required, you'll be able to harmonize folk-style bass and melody lines.

 **TRACK 47/1**

EXERCISE I
Country-inspired lick in G. Take care to avoid picking the B string until the D in the final bar.

Exercise I features a chromatic lick that sounds great over a I–IV–V–I progression. Shown here in G, it forms a movable shape suitable for any major key.

Also in G, Exercise II features a Spanish-influenced double-stop lick that harmonizes with a I–II–I progression, with notes picked from the triads of those chords, together with sixths, which are picked here but would sound equally great as a slide. Meanwhile, Exercise III is written with a I–IV–V–I progression in mind. It's in B♭, which gives it a jaunty Chuck Berry–style feel.

EXERCISE II

This lick shows how easy it is to build double-stop riffs and licks starting with the notes within the chord.

```
T |------------------------7----5----|---3----3----3----5----7--|
A |--4----4----4-----------7----5----|---4----4----4----5----7--|
B |--5----5----5---------------------|--------------------------|

  |--5----5----5----9----5---|---4----------------------|
  |--7----7----7----7----7---|---5----------------------|
  |--------------------------|--------------------------|
```

EXERCISE III

Both this and the previous lick will sound great with vibrato added across all of the notes, adding some authentic "shake, rattle, and roll!"

```
T |-------11----------|-------------------|-------------------|----9----10----11--|
A |-10-10-10-10-10----|-10-10-10-10-------|-10-10-10-8---7----|----8----9-----10--|
B |-12-12-12----12----|-10-10--8----8-----|-12-12-12-10--8----|-------------------|
```

Chuck Berry–Style
Riffs and Licks

This Missouri-born showman developed a guitar style that helped to distinguish rock 'n' roll from rhythm and blues, and his trademark licks were a major influence on British blues-boom guitarists such as Keith Richards (see pages 160 and 161). An inveterate tourer, Berry would often travel alone, playing with "pick-up" bands recruited from among the best musicians in each city he visited, which shows how universal his music had become.

Berry's lyrics often celebrated the freedom and travel made possible by the automobile, and his music reflects their sense of motion, often by playing "straight eights" (simple quaver beats) against swing-based rhythm parts, evoking the sound of a car engine—even with their name! In the first exercise, ringing double-stops simply emphasize the major and minor thirds, deriving interest from their triplet rhythm, another Chuck Berry staple. Here, they are shown in B♭, voiced against a dominant seventh tonic chord.

This exercise is an example of a riff with a straight-eight rhythm. Alternating between the fifths and sixths of each chord, it's similar to a shuffle lick, but you'll notice the difference in timing as you play it. Shown in B♭, it contains no thirds and so is neither major nor minor.

Sixths also feature in the following exercise. Here they're voiced, once again, as a Berry-style double stop alternated against the fifth in his trademark shuffle rhythm.

"If you tried to give rock 'n' roll another name, you might call it Chuck Berry."

TRACK 48

John Lennon

EXERCISE I
Derived from the top two notes of the tonic dominant seventh chord, this lick works equally well over the tonic or major chord.

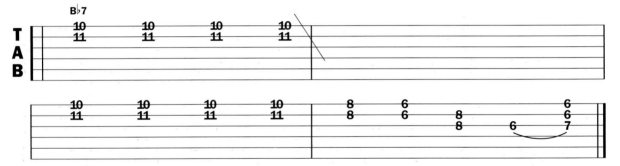

Chuck Berry

With quick-witted lyrics full of cars and girls, Chuck Berry laid the groundwork for not only a rock 'n' roll sound but a rock 'n' roll worldview. While no single person can lay claim to inventing rock 'n' roll, Berry comes closest of all, as he was the one to put all the essential ingredients together. His ingenious graft of country and western guitar licks on rhythm and blues in his first single, "Maybellene," with its brief but scorching guitar solo and his trademark double-string licks, created a sound for the future.

TRIPLET RHYTHMS

Chuck Berry may have considered himself an entertainer first and foremost, but he was also a hugely influential guitarist, most notably on the Beatles and The Rolling Stones. Berry pioneered triplet rhythms for the guitar, in which there are three beats for every beat of the bar. Often used with double-stops, such as notes 1 and 4 of the scale, they're best played with a down-up-down stroke pattern.

TRACK 49

EXERCISE II

These power-chord voicings contain no third. They're shown forming the "turnaround" bars of a twelve-bar blues.

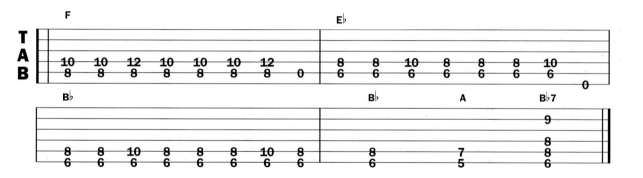

Scotty Moore–Style Licks

**As guitarist on Elvis Presley's most immortal hits, such as "That's Alright (Mama)," "Hound Dog,"
and "Jailhouse Rock," Scotty Moore's spare, country-influenced lead picking provided the perfect foil
to "The King's" rock 'n' roll baritone. Reserved on stage, Moore was, in effect, the first dedicated lead
guitarist outside of a swing band—B.B. King and Chuck Berry had had hit records by the time Elvis
became popular in 1954 but were all-round performers foremost, though we think of them today for
their guitar styles.**

Moore was reunited with Presley for his '68 Comeback
Special, concert footage of which shows off his raw,
down-home lead picking to great effect.

Exercise I here features an open lick in A, and
emphasizes the sixth and ninth. Similarly major, this lick
is also one to be played over the tonic chord, this time in
E, and also emphasizes the sixth (C#).

Moore's licks often alternated between bars in which
he repeated the vocal melody, and banjo rolls—the
repetition of a chromatic slide against an open string,
such as the one in Exercise II below.

This two-bar lick—shown here in G and played to
best effect over a tonic dominant seventh or major
chord—is a great way to end a solo or song. By the
mid-1970s, punk rockers, reacting to the excesses of
extended prog rock pieces, sought to rediscover licks
like these. With overdrive, this would have been as at
home in the back room of a north London pub as it
was in Tennessee.

Scotty Moore was fluent in jazz and country music.
His riffs are informed by them and are deceptive in
their simplicity.

 **TRACK 50**

EXERCISE I
This two-bar riff requires dexterity with your picking hand, as it involves skipping
strings. This adds a major sixth, ninth, and major seventh to the tonic chord.

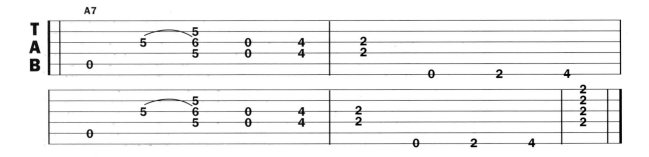

Scotty Moore

With his early background in jazz and country, Scotty Moore put these influences to use counterpointing Presley's vocals with melodic yet forceful solos—a sound that helped to launch the rockabilly revolution and brought the first sounds of rock 'n' roll to life. Colin Escott, music writer and journalist, wrote of Moore, "The first generation of kids who grew up wanting to play rock 'n' roll cut their teeth on Scotty Moore's solo." This was confirmed by The Rolling Stones's guitarist Keith Richards, who said, "Everyone else wanted to be Elvis; I wanted to be Scotty."

> **"Rock 'n' roll music, if you like it, if you feel it—you can't help but move to it. That's what happens to me. I can't help it."**
>
> *Elvis Presley*

 TRACK 51

EXERCISE II

This lick adds the sixth to the tonic major chord and moves from the minor third to the major third (G/G#).

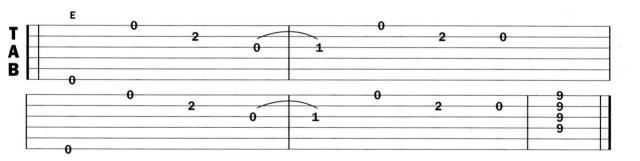

Your First
Rock 'n' Roll Song

In the 1950s, the rock 'n' roll scene was brimming with teenage talents such as Buddy Holly and Eddie Cochran. Artists would cut their own vinyl singles in the hopes of getting them played on America's local radio stations, building enough local attention to drive them to national success.

Those artists who were signed to large record labels, however, were often paired with studio bands whose guitarists had jazz and country music backgrounds. These artists brought their licks to the party, adding color and inflection to simple, driving chord progressions derived from jump bands or the blues.

The following song consists of three parts, with its key center in Dm. In the verse, the Dm-scale lead part is a damped version of the one that follows in the refrain, while the chorus opens out into a more spacious feel. It makes use of a common and much-loved cadence, the kind of driving, descending progression that inspired the early Beatles.

TRACK 52

Buddy Holly
Despite having a period of success that lasted a mere 18 months before his death in a plane crash, Buddy Holly became the pioneer and the face of rock 'n' roll. Critic Bruce Elder described Holly as "the single most influential creative force in early rock 'n' roll." His works, including the timeless classics "Oh Boy," "Peggy Sue," "That'll Be the Day," and "Not Fade Away," inspired and influenced many great artists who followed, including the Beatles, The Rolling Stones, Don McLean, and Bob Dylan, and his influence on modern music has been equally profound and wide reaching.

REFRAIN

VERSE

CHORUS

Play Classic Rock

America—with its many driver-friendly radio stations and stadium-sized concerts—is the home of classic rock today. But in the 1960s, it was British guitarists, bored with the limitations of "skiffle" music—jazz, blues, and folk-based music with country influences, often played on homemade or improvised instruments—who began to copy the guitar parts from imported U.S. blues LPs by artists such as Howlin' Wolf. Chicago blues—the electrified, urban version of acoustic, rural blues from the Mississippi Delta—provided the template for sonic experiments by the pioneers of the British blues boom.

Two London bands in particular, The Yardbirds and John Mayall's Bluesbreakers, became revolving doors for the mercurial talents of Eric Clapton, Jeff Beck, and Jimmy Page. These blues-boom bands mutated through psychedelia into rock giants such as Cream and, of course, Led Zeppelin. Meanwhile, another London blues-boom band had been persuaded by their record company to spell their name with a "g," and The Rollin' Stones never looked back.

Other blues-influenced rock bands, such as Free and The Pretty Things, made for a thriving 1960s/1970s music scene in which the likes of Deep Purple took rock musicianship to new heights and audiences. The following chapter outlines the techniques that took them there and teaches the rudiments of rock that retains the warmth and melodic content of the blues, while laying the mammoth foundations of heavy metal.

Gibson SG

The Gibson SG has a shallower body than the Gibson Les Paul, making it much lighter. It is a favorite of many players, including Black Sabbath's Tony Iommi, Eric Clapton, and Derek Trucks of The Allman Brothers Band.

Useful Chord Progressions
for Classic Rock

We've discussed how classic rock has its roots in the blues. Therefore, it's useful to start your thinking about the possibilities of blues-rock in terms of further things that can be done with a twelve-bar blues progression (see pages 74 and 75).

The Roman-numeral chord charts on this page can be used with the chord shapes from pages 24, 25, 30, and 31, together with the fifth-chord voicings used in the previous two chapters, to suit any key.

It's worth knowing some common variations of the simple twelve-bar. The following are derived from the early pioneering work of the early Delta blues musicians, so they're progressions that should sound familiar. Jam through them in two or three popular keys—E, A, and B or G, C, and D—so that you can hear the differences in tension and resolution between them. On the next pages, we'll see how they can provide the building blocks for more varied classic-rock tracks that draw on these progressions even when using power chords and single-note runs (or especially, given that classic shuffle riffs such as Chuck Berry's—see pages 100 and 101—are fifth chords too).

"Quick-four" variation using subdominant in second bar:

I–IV–I–I
IV–IV–I–I
V–IV–I–I

Dominant chord through the tenth bar:

I–I–I–I
IV–IV–I–I
V–V–I–I

Ritchie Blackmore
Blackmore is an English guitarist and founding member of the hard rock bands Deep Purple and Rainbow. Deep Purple's greatest hit, "Smoke on the Water," features one of Blackmore's best-known guitar riffs, which he plays without a pick, using two fingers to pluck the strings in fourths. The riff has become a must-learn piece for beginners to rock-guitar playing. Blackmore was ranked No. 55 in *Rolling Stone* magazine's "100 Greatest Guitarists of All Time."

"I actually play very lightly."

Ritchie Blackmore (Deep Purple)

Exercise I shows you a further twist to the twelve bar, with harmonized sevenths—these are different from major sevenths (see pages 156 and 157) in being dominant sevenths (a whole tone, rather than a semitone, below the octave).

Exercise II adds another popular "color" note by substituting ninth chords in addition to the sevenths above. Similarly, these are dominant ninths, a second above the octave. Note how they sound different than sharp ninths—the famous "Hendrix chord" (see pages 158 and 159)—which feature a minor third above the octave and have a more mellow, jazzy sound. Nevertheless, they're still a common passing note in classic rock tunes.

TRACK 53/1

EXERCISE I

Twelve-bar progressions remain common in classic rock. This simple progression in A oscillates major chords with their dominant sevenths. Upstrokes on the "and 3" beats will help you maintain rhythm.

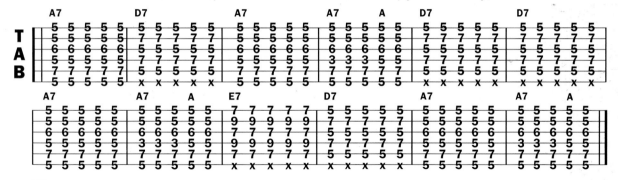

TRACK 53/2

EXERCISE II

Ninth chords substituted in a similar way to the sevenths above, again in A. These sounds often occur in classic rock lead lines too, played against fifth power chords.

Classic Rock
Chord Progressions

The following chord progressions are representative of common sequences that occur in classic rock (and, for that matter, music from punk onward). They're designed simply to give you a sense of the ease with which chord progressions can be constructed from the diatonic chords built on the major scales (see pages 22 and 23).

 TRACK 54/1

EXERCISE I

Simple I–V–I progressions are common in classic rock. This one is embellished with a sus4, in A.

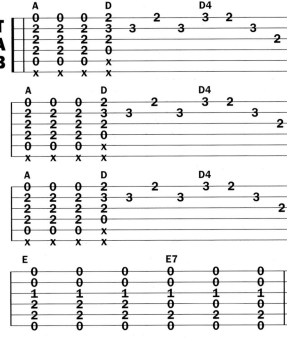

J.J. Cale
American singer-songwriter J.J.Cale pioneered the fluid, laid-back country-blues shuffles that led the way for Mark Knopfler and Eric Clapton. A pioneer of the "Tulsa sound," a laid-back blend of rock 'n' roll, country, folk, blues, and jazz, Cale's songs include the rock standards "After Midnight" and "Cocaine." All his songs feature astonishing, delicate, and intricate guitar work, but the best also contain an irresistible melodic hook.

Chords are still implied, even if the styles you like do not involve strummed chords, but riffs and chord fragments. So a knowledge of the tonality (major or minor) of the chords built on the major scale will equip you with the ability to start constructing songs and progressions beyond the twelve-bar right away.

TRACK 54/2

EXERCISE II

This exercise explores other chords in A, beginning with the sixth. It would therefore form a suitable alternating verse or chorus part for the preceding exercise.

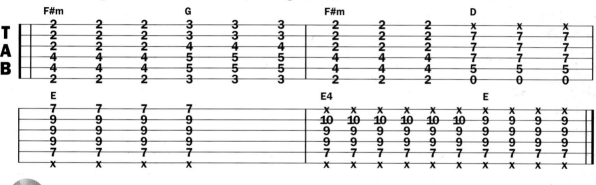

TRACK 54/3

EXERCISE III

A classic-rock ballad-style progression in C. The ascending major-chord run at the end would resolve to a tonic-based chorus or verse part.

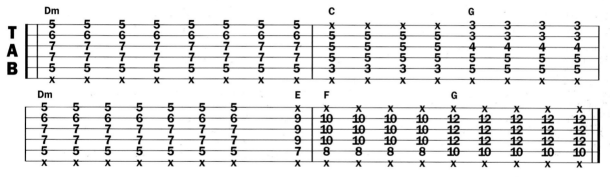

Easy Blues
Rock Riffs

The appeal of blues rock lies in its imaginative riffs and licks—if not simply a twelve bar, then its underlying chord progressions are often fairly straightforward in themselves. The following riffs show off just some of the exciting things that can be done with an underlying chord progression that might otherwise be quite familiar.

TRACK 55/1

EXERCISE I

Despite the pretense of the minor third (C) in this riff, it remains strong and harmonically ambiguous thanks to the fifth-chord voicings.

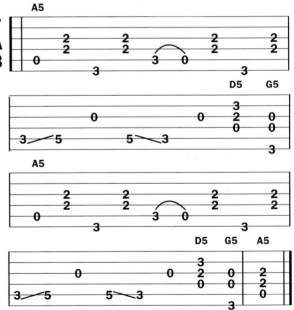

Paul Kossoff
Respected soulful, bluesy, rock guitarist Kossoff was best known as a member of the 1970's British band Free. Their massive hit single, "All Right Now," became a classic rock standard. Renowned for his fluid, slow, and melodic leads and bluesy riffs, "Koss" ranked No. 51 in *Rolling Stone* magazine's list of the "100 Greatest Guitarists of All Time."

These riffs either imply the tension and resolution of their underlying chords or else exploit the harmonic ambiguity that derives from omitting the third note of the scale (in the case of the second riff).

TRACK 55/2

EXERCISE II

A blues scale–based classic rock–style solo. Played power trio–style (without accompaniment), it is harmonically ambiguous.

TRACK 55/3

EXERCISE III

Power chords with ambiguous tonalities are contrasted with major chords. The D chord is inverted with its fifth in the bass (see pages 48 and 49).

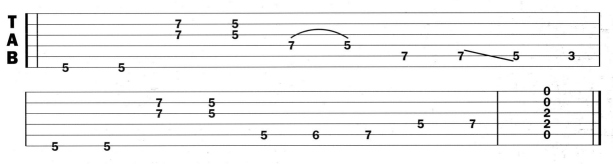

Out-There
Solos

During the era of classic rock, guitar solos began to borrow ideas from outside of the blues-inspired techniques covered in Chapter 4. By the early 1970s, rock guitarists had begun drawing on a wider range of intervals than the blues. Pioneering guitarist John McLaughlin formed the hugely influential Mahavishnu Orchestra in 1971, and jazz-rock fusion was born. An understanding of the techniques used by fusion guitarists will broaden your resources and allow you to incorporate "out-there" sounds in your solos. You can begin to mix more complex harmony with heaviness with just a handful of techniques that are no harder to grasp than major and minor scales.

The diminished scale consists of: root–2–♭3–4–♭5–♭6–6–7. Because of its alternate tone-semitone intervals, it has four key centers—first, third, fifth, and seventh—so three diminished scales are all you need to cover all twelve keys:

C—matches E♭, G♭, A
C#—matches E, G, B♭
D—matches F, A♭, B

Or:

E—G, B♭, D♭
F—A♭, B, D
F# —A, C, E♭

. . . and so on through the chromatic scale. The diminished comes easily to the fingers thanks to its alternate tone-semitone pattern.

Another symmetric (one that divides the octave into equal parts) scale is the augmented, or whole-tone scale.

TRACK 56

EXERCISE I

Diminished scale used over a minor-to-major progression: Em and B7 alternate in the first half, moving to D and its dominant A7.

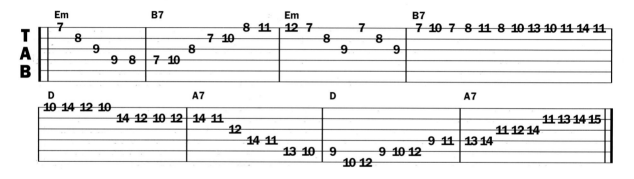

Since it consists simply of whole tones (every other semitone), only two whole-tone scales, a semitone apart, are needed to cover all twelve keys. It's a dominant scale that can be used over dominant sevenths.

Diminished and augmented scales predate the major and minor tonalities inherent in our modern musical thinking. Which is why they have an off-the-wall, "outside" sound in the context of blues-derived music, with its heavy emphasis on what the third is doing. Since they disrupt the tonality, you are unlikely to stay on them for long. But, used to link two scale types together, they create a great harmonic "wake-up call."

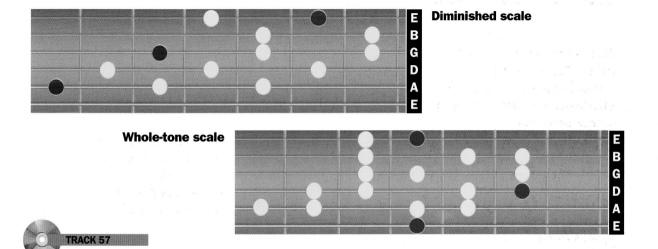

Diminished scale

E
B
G
D
A
E

Whole-tone scale

E
B
G
D
A
E

TRACK 57

EXERCISE II

Whole-tone scale used against a Bm to E9 progression with a funk groove. The ninth voicing avoids the fifth, which would sound dissonant against the sharp fifth of the scale.

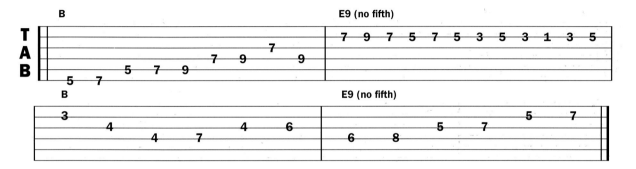

Classic Rock–Style Solo

Our featured solo includes several distinctive elements that make classic rock pieces so rewarding to play. It's picked against the chord progression from the classic rock tune on the following pages, and aims to provide a great starting point for incorporating some of the essential licks and phrases of melodic rock soloing into your playing. Solo along to this twelve-bar riff in G, and you should begin to gain a feel for incorporating some of these tried-and-tested licks and phrases into your playing.

Our solo uses the minor blues scale (the minor pentatonic with an added flat fifth; see page 61), against a rhythm part that consists of power-chord fifths—there are no thirds or color notes to inhibit your choice of notes from this scale. In combination with the tab, you can use the scale patterns on page 62.

TRACK 58

Classic Rock's Power

Led Zeppelin's "Stairway to Heaven"—the most played song on radio never to have been released as a single—Queen's "Bohemian Rhapsody," Aerosmith's "Dream On," The Rolling Stones's "Brown Sugar," Steppenwolf's "Born to be Wild," and the Eagles's "Hotel California" are all classic rock epics. The breadth of classic rock is huge, with something for every listening taste, but the impact was even greater, moving popular music from the warmth of blues to the sheer visceral power of heavy metal. From the ballad to the guitar-thrashing arena song, classic rock's power in music is an ongoing legacy of immense popularity.

David Gilmour
Pink Floyd guitarist Gilmour's guitar playing and songwriting became major factors of Floyd's worldwide success during the 1970s. His distinctive vocals and playing on *The Dark Side of the Moon* helped it to become the third most successful selling album of all time.

SOLO

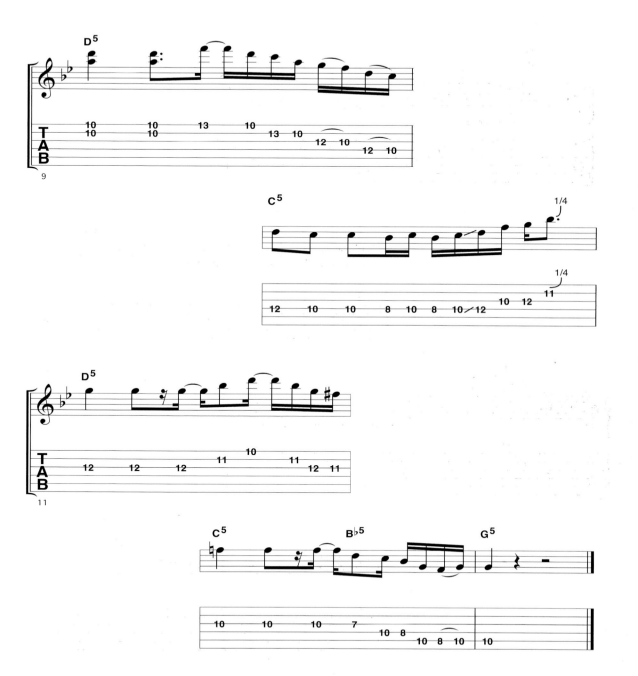

Your First Classic Rock Song

Our classic-rock track has three parts, each of which uses the techniques of early 1970s heavy rock bands. It has a groove that would have been at home in a Led Zeppelin or Free track. Hear how its dynamism partly derives from the snare drum used on the offbeat before the fourth beat of the bar.

The main verse part in G features strident fifth-chord voicings, with another verse part featuring a less expansive single-note riff. The latter is the kind of passage that could function as a break after the second chorus. The third part modulates to D (the dominant of G), providing a strong chorus riff.

Jamming through this piece should show you just how easy it is to play often-heard riffing patterns such as these. Featured techniques include hammer-ons and slides (of single notes and fifth chords), quarter-tone bends, and single-note vibrato. Add these rhythm riffs to your guitar arsenal, and you have a firm harmonic basis on which to try out your solo ideas.

 TRACK 59

Great Rock Riffs

Some of the most memorable, recognizable, haunting, and oft-repeated riffs come from the great classic rock staples. Songs such as AC/DC's "Back in Black," Led Zeppelin's "Heartbreaker," Black Sabbath's "Iron Man," and Hendrix's "Purple Haze," have riffs that have outshone the songs themselves in their popular appeal and worldwide recognition. Others, like Thin Lizzy's "The Boys Are Back in Town" and Deep Purple's "Smoke on the Water," have paved the way for hundreds of would-be songwriters to create such iconic sounds that keep people returning year after year to the classic rock masterpieces.

Slash
In 1988, Guns N' Roses had their first No. 1 hit with "Sweet Child o' Mine," a song that hangs on Slash's masterful classic rock riff and guitar solo. His energizing playing and memorable riffs helped GNR's *Appetite for Destruction* become the best-selling debut album of all time.

PART I

PART 2

CHORUS

Play Heavy Metal

The phrase is thought to have come from "Born to Be Wild" by the band Steppenwolf, which describes the sound of big motorcycles with the line "heavy-metal thunder." Metal music has always found fans in the foundries and factories of industrial areas, from America's heartland to Birmingham in the UK and the cities of Germany's Ruhr valley.

From the late 1970s, UK bands such as Iron Maiden and Def Leppard revisited the sounds of classic rock bands such as Deep Purple and sought to make them heavier. Meanwhile, in California, bands such as Motley Crüe introduced an element of glam and sleaze. Next, bands like Anthrax and Slayer picked up on the punk frenzy (as Motörhead had done in the UK) and incorporated speeded-up riffs and breakneck beats. Drop-dead shredding solos and speed metal from the likes of Dragonforce have followed.

The following chapter reveals the techniques that make metal what it is today and takes a wrecking ball to classic heavy rock passages, exposing their foundations to show you the tricks involved.

Jackson Randy Rhoads

The Jackson Randy Rhoads electric guitar was originally commissioned by Ozzy Osbourne's guitarist Randy Rhoads, who wanted a guitar that resembled a shark's fin, before his untimely death in a plane crash. A student of classical guitar, Rhoads often combined classical influences with his heavy metal style. Famous players include Kirk Hammett of Metallica, Phil Campbell of Motörhead, and Adrian Smith of Iron Maiden.

Smooth
Harmonics

By no means exclusive to metal, harmonics have nonetheless become an essential part of the axe-wielding shred guitar player's arsenal, and that's where they're currently heard most often. Eddie Van Halen (see pages 140–141) is the preeminent exponent of the technique and incorporates them cohesively into melodies and riffs, rather than including them as an afterthought to fill the remaining part of a bar.

Once the preserve of clean-toned players such as George Harrison (whose solo on the Beatles' "Nowhere Man" is a satisfying tour de force), they are in fact easier to accomplish with high-gain metal sounds, in which saturated distortion can even out the differences of volume between harmonics and fretted notes, especially with compression.

The sound by which we identify the pitch of a note is only the loudest element of the sound we hear. At the same time as it produces this "fundamental," the string is vibrating in shorter loops, producing a series of overtones known as "harmonics." It is the blend of the fundamental and harmonics in relation to each other that produces the very tone of your guitar. Since the laws of nature require absolute precision, no two instruments, however mass-produced, will ever have exactly the same tone.

The twelfth fret is halfway along the vibrating part of your guitar strings and produces a harmonic an octave above the fundamental. Dividing each string length into three, over the seventh or nineteenth fret, will produce a harmonic three times higher than the fundamental—an octave and a fifth above, and so on, until they become too high for the human ear to hear.

Sound a harmonic by positioning the tip of your index finger directly over the fret, not just behind it, as you do when fretting it conventionally. Do not depress the string to the fret but touch it lightly. Lift your finger from the string as fast as you can in the moment *after* you have picked it. Harmonics require perseverance and practice with your fretting hand. But once you have cracked the technique it will be second nature.

FRETTED-NOTE HARMONICS

The fun starts once you are playing open-string harmonics confidently, with harmonics generated above fretted notes. This requires a technique from your picking hand that is similar to two-handed tapping (see pages 132 and 133) but crucially different in that you are sounding the harmonic with your picking hand at an upper fret, rather than fretting the upper fret.

Let's say you want to pick an open G chord as first harmonics, so it'll sound an octave above the fretted note (Exercise I). Hold the pick between your thumb and second finger and, holding your hand rigid, extend your first finger to fret the harmonic with its pad. Just as you do when playing an open-string harmonic with your fretting hand, pick the note as you hold your first finger against the string and then remove it in the next instant.

OPEN-STRING HARMONICS

Harmonic	Interval above fundamental	Fret
1st harmonic	octave	12
2nd harmonic	octave+5th	7, 19
3rd harmonic	2 octaves	5, 24
4th harmonic	2 octaves+maj 3rd	4, 9, 16
5th harmonic	2 octaves+5th	$3\frac{1}{3}$

Fretting our open G chord with your fretting hand in the normal way, sound a harmonic with your picking hand as above on the fifteenth fret of the low E string, fourteenth fret of the A string, the twelfth fret of the open D, G, and B strings, and the fifteenth fret of the top E string. Voila! This one chord will show you that you can play any chord this way if its highest-fretted note (as opposed to the most high-pitched) is located at the ninth or below on a 21-fret neck, tenth on a 22-fret, and the full twelve on a 24-fret neck. Simply pick the harmonic directly over the fret an octave above. Watch out for open and fretted harmonics in the exercises in this chapter.

TRACK 60/1

EXERCISE I

Fretted harmonics picking on an open G arpeggio.

TRACK 60/2

EXERCISE II

D, A, and G major arpeggios picked with fretted harmonics. Compression or distortion will add sustain and help you master this tricky technique.

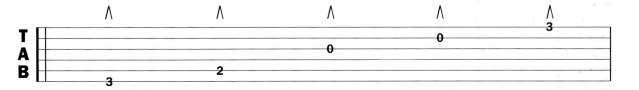

Easy Drop-D Tuning
Power Chord Riffs

By now it should be apparent that many of the "rules" of rock exist to make things easier, however complex they sound. Dropped-D tuning, or drop-D, is one of these. It simply means that the bottom E string is tuned down a whole tone to D, making the tuning DADGBE.

The three bass strings are now tuned to a D5, the power chord consisting of root, fifth, and octave. Played with the pad of the index finger as a movable shape, these three strings are powerful heavy-metal tools, adding plangent, often-distorted bass-string tones while allowing for very fast changes.

Drop-D tuning began as a fingerpicking technique, allowing players to keep an alternating bass part going when playing in the popular folk key of D. But slides using the three bass strings are surprisingly smooth and accurate compared with how damping is usually preferable when changing chord shapes. And of course all the familiar movable chords with roots on the A string are still there for you, while many open-string voicings require little adaptation.

DROP-D
Drop-D tuning allows you to slide whole riffs! Have fun building power-chord riffs with root notes from any scale you choose. Because of the uncomplicated fifth harmonies, you can slide semitonal intervals, or hammer on whole-tone intervals, with the time values of passing notes. Open-string licks are easily incorporated, as in Exercise II.

TRACK 61/1

EXERCISE I

A neo-classical riff based on minor arpeggios in F. Note how the whole power chord is slid during the final bar.

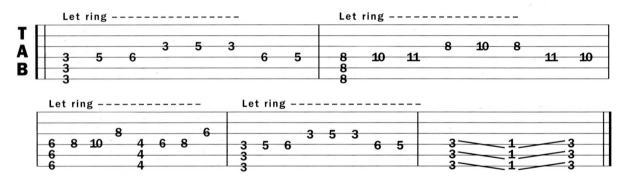

Kerry King

Slayer guitarist Kerry King's playing is often more focused on speed and chaos than melody. However, his unfaltering playing style has given King a very distinctive sound. His strong rhythm work aside, he also has a distinctive and unique lead guitar style that some have called "grab the guitar neck and hang from the whammy bar as if your life depends on it." However, despite this, it must be said that King has almost singlehandedly created an entirely new style of soloing and influenced countless thrash and death-metal bands.

> **There's no point having one tuning for just one song. So, we got like two 7-string tunings, we got four dropped to B, and the rest of the record is in D sharp.**
>
> *Kerry King* (Slayer) on drop tuning on the album *Speaking In Tongues*

 **TRACK 61/2**

EXERCISE II

A simple power-chord riff in E (moving to G, the minor third) is made even easier thanks to drop-D tuning, allowing you to make barres with your first and fourth fingers.

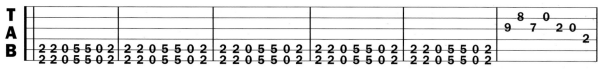

Easy Two-Handed
Tapping Licks

These days, nothing says you're into playing the guitar like a mastery of tapping techniques. The first popular tapping piece of recent history was Eddie Van Halen's "Eruption," which remains a state-of-the-art showcase of the style. Invariably, it is two-handed tapping you will hear about most, but we can explain the idea with reference to one-handed tapping first. Tapping can be applied to any note. It involves sounding the second note in a phrase by tapping the first or second finger (ninety-nine per cent of the time, though complex polyphonic taps using all four fingers are also possible) of your picking hand just behind a fret farther up the fretboard on that same string, typically above the twelfth fret.

Two-handed tapping means combining this with hammer-ons and pull-offs played with your fretting hand. Where one-handed tapping produces diads, two-handed tapping produces triad phrases, or even more. Coordinating the fingers of both hands closely, you can produce trills that work in triads, arpeggios, and other intervals. Thanks to the very wide intervals that tapping techniques make use of, they can produce some exciting, otherworldly sounds suitable for symphonic epics, or a science fiction concept album.

Imagine you are striking a piano key with your picking hand. Work on developing sufficient control to fret the new note firmly enough so that you can release it quickly, having sounded it cleanly, or sustain it for longer if desired, even adding vibrato with a firm, gentle up-and-down motion of the tapping finger. This is a legato style, so you want to produce smooth tones that run into each other.

Some players prefer to tap with the pad of their first finger, some with their second. It depends on how you can best become "quick on the draw" in getting your pick

TRACK 62/1

EXERCISE I

This major arpeggio in B features a hammered-on fourth. Practice removing the fourth finger of your fretting hand from the seventh fret just as you have tapped the twelfth with your picking hand.

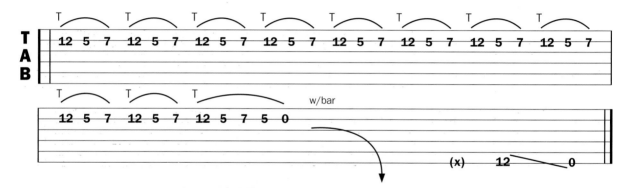

Buckethead
American musician, songwriter, and guitar virtuoso, Buckethead is famed for his distinctive stage outfit and amazing playing speed. Although he replaced Slash in Guns N' Roses for a while, Buckethead has released 29 solo albums, performed on more than 50 others, and made guest appearances on more than 40 different albums by various artists. His music spans such diverse areas as progressive metal, thrash metal, funk, electronica, jazz, bluegrass, and avant-garde, and he was voted No. 8 on a list in *GuitarOne* magazine of the "Top 20 Greatest Guitar Shredders of All Time."

out of the way. Some players tap with the edge of their pick, but most either tuck their pick further into their palm with their second finger and thumb, or simply extend their second finger and tap with that, which feels a little less natural at first, but which makes for faster incorporation of the technique within a series of picked notes.

Mastering tapping requires very well-developed hand coordination. However, if it sounds rather daunting, you may find your technique takes off once you apply saturated distortion tones.

TRACK 62/2

EXERCISE II

An eerie minor lick in D that moves between the fifth and sharp fifth.

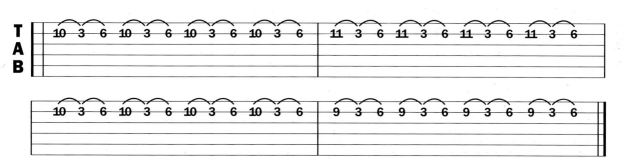

Led Zeppelin–Style
Riffs and Licks

Born from the ashes of The Yardbirds, Led Zeppelin's mighty rock career spanned the 1970s. Their monolithic bass and drum patterns were an inspiration to hip-hop—the sampled drum introduction to "When the Levée Breaks" from _Led Zep IV_ provided the backbeat to many rap hits of the 1990s, keeping their legacy alive and reincorporated into developing pop culture.

"Zep" are famous for their high-impact pyrotechnics, riffs, and flashy solos, but while guitarist Jimmy Page is famous for wielding his Les Paul or Gibson SG twin neck on stage, he was also a thoughtful studio musician, creating texture with acoustics, Telecasters, and electric twelve-strings.

Exercise I feels like a riff from the late 1960s or early 1970s. Shown here in A, you'll see that the major third is not stated, in true power-chord riff fashion. The second bar observes a strict sixteenth-beat (semiquaver) rhythm that sounds great over a laid back Bonham-style beat.

The exercise features a simple, aggressive riff that leaves space for some dramatic, John Bonham–style drum fills. Since Led Zeppelin was a single-guitar band, it fell to Jimmy Page to establish both harmony and melody, and to imply chords in his riffs where they weren't explicitly stated. Here, a G-major pentatonic riff alternates with a A5 power chord.

Page played many showy, bravura licks that made use of the sixths. The sixth appears in the major pentatonic scale and introduces major tonality to a power-chord riff (shown here in the rock-friendly key of E). Exercise II is representative of one of Page's sixth licks, and shows the influence on his playing of country and rock 'n' roll, requiring accurate whole-tone string bends.

TRACK 63

EXERCISE I

An A5 followed by a G-major pentatonic riff. G is the ♭VII chord of root scale A, not voiced here but implied by the notes of the riff.

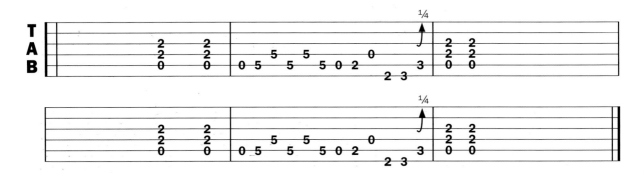

Jimmy Page

With their heavy, guitar-driven blues-rock sound, Led Zeppelin are regularly cited as one of the progenitors of heavy metal and hard rock music. Described as "unquestionably one of the all-time most influential, important, and versatile guitarists and songwriters in rock history," guitarist Jimmy Page was ranked No. 9 in *Rolling Stone* magazine's "100 Greatest Guitarists of All Time."

FRETTING STYLE

Jimmy Page's fretting style, featuring percussive short notes and fretting-hand damping, helped him to come up with simple iconic riffs, such as that in "Whole Lotta Love." Many of his most famous riffs feature just four or even three notes. His sound has stood the test of time: Puff Daddy's "Come With Me," featuring Page's "Kashmir" riff, shows that the song really does remain the same.

TRACK 64

EXERCISE II

Major-sixth and major-pentatonic riff in E. The lead line imposes its tonality on the harmonically ambiguous fifths.

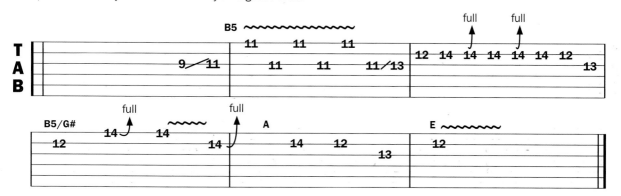

Black Sabbath–Style Riffs and Licks

Black Sabbath hit their doom-laden stride at the beginning of the 1970s. Early stadium rockers, they pioneered hitherto unheard levels of amplification and found fame in their native UK and the US. Classic tracks such as "Paranoid" and "Iron Man" emphasize heavy riffing over virtuosity, and the accessibility of their riffs has been one reason for their enduring popularity.

Alienated working-class lads, they had no airs and graces, and their music has a lack of pretense that's unique outside of punk bands. In the same way that learning Ramones progressions will have you playing whole songs in no time, picking up some Black Sabbath–style riffs is a relatively fast way to having some effective changes at your fingertips.

In order to compensate for a hand injury, guitarist Tony Iommi pioneered the drop-tuned guitar styles that have influenced today's metal bands—and even the development of seven-string guitars—with churning, cyclic riffs. Iommi used drop-D tuning (see pages 130 and 131), but his preferred tuning is known as "drop minor third" tuning, which involves tuning each string one and a half

tones below standard tuning. This has the advantage of allowing you to play familiar chord shapes, so that an A major chord, for example, is formed by a conventional C shape, and so on for all other chords, as per the transposition chart on page 33.

These exercises, however, are given in standard tuning. Exercise I makes use of the infamous tritone—the diminished fifth, banned from church music during the Middle Ages. Full of portent, it's the interval that is repeated at the start of Jimi Hendrix's "Purple Haze." This four-bar movable riff is played here in C#, beginning on the low E string—Iommi often used chord voicings that are played on the lower strings around the middle of the neck, for their mid-range tonal qualities. This exercise also

Major Influence

Black Sabbath have influenced nu-metal, grunge and, before them, American hardcore, as evidenced by the Butthole Surfers's "Sweat Loaf," a cheeky homage to Sabbath's "Sweet Leaf."

Paul Leary
Butthole Surfers guitarist Paul Leary's music is founded in hardcore punk with a sound that incorporates elements of Sabbath's accessibility.

features the tritone of C#, G, as a passing fifth chord on the way to the dominant.

Exercise II demonstrates a frequent Iommi technique: many Black Sabbath riffs are simple two-note power chord fifths. The first bar, meanwhile, features hammer-ons for increased speed.

TRACK 65

EXERCISE I

"Tritone" (♭5) power-chord riff in C#. The interval refers to the root scale on which the chords are built.

SETTING THE TONE

GAIN   BASS   MIDDLE   TREBLE   VOLUME

Tonally, Black Sabbath could have inspired the *Spinal Tap* scene in which lead guitarist Nigel Tufnel states that all of his amplifier controls "go all the way up to eleven." In practice, set your gain at the point where sustained single notes are on the point of feeding back, before adjusting your master volume to the level your overall band mix requires.

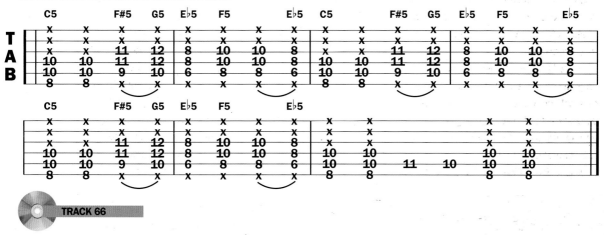

TRACK 66

EXERCISE II

Power-chord riff in A introduced by a simple hammered-on run that uses the fourth and sixth.

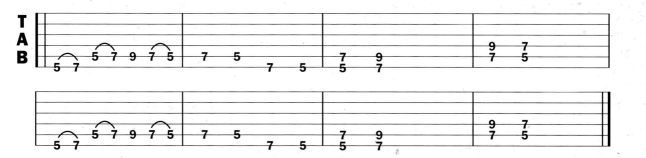

AC/DC-Style
Riffs and Licks

Angus Young, founding member and lead guitarist of these Australian rockers, has been touring the world, performing in his trademark schoolboy's uniform, for over thirty-five years. Filed under "metal," their music is really a kind of overdriven barroom blues, featuring plenty of pentatonic and blues scale–based soloing, but with six-string voicings that make fifth chords expansive enough to fill stadiums.

Strutting from one side of the stage to the other with his animated version of Chuck Berry's "duck walk," Angus Young took a large share in fronting the band, especially following the death of original vocalist Bon Scott. Musically, however, the AC/DC sound is a careful blend of Angus's sparse, effective lead phrases, and brother Malcolm's rock-solid rhythm playing. The brothers Young will often hit two different voicings of the same chord—a big factor in the characteristically "chunky" sound of classics such as "Touch too Much" or "You Shook Me all Night Long," perfect for the band's swaggering tales of sexual exploits, real or imagined.

SETTING THE TONE

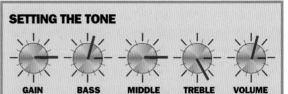

| GAIN | BASS | MIDDLE | TREBLE | VOLUME |

Angus Young opts for overdriven "crunch" tones, rather than the saturated distortion you might expect, with enough clean tone in his sound for each note to be heard discretely. For a Gibson player, his tone is relatively trebly and cuts through the mix.

TRACK 67

EXERCISE I

Fretting the open D5 shape with your first and third fingers allows you to bring your second over to fret the C on the A string in the main part of this riff.

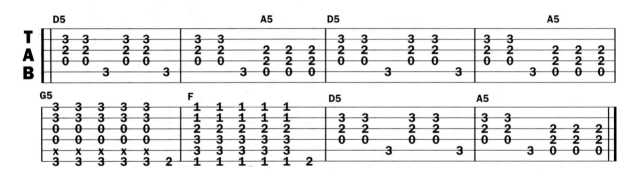

66**We never thought of ourselves as a heavy metal band—we've always regarded ourselves as a rock band. The big difference: we've always thought we had a lot more feel for rock, we always went out for songs, not riffs or heavy, heavy sounds. But every now and again it does come on like a sledgehammer.**99

Angus Young (AC/DC)

Exercise I contains an eight-bar riff. Note how the C in the bass adds blues-scale interest in the first four bars, since it's the minor seventh of the D5 chord and the minor third of the A5. In the second four bars, the F# chromatic passing note between the G5 and F-major barre is the major third of D and the major sixth of A, establishing tonality and linking the two halves of this cyclic riff.

In Exercise II, it's left to the rhythm guitar (if present) to state tonality while the lead plays a power-chord riff.

The A in the first bar features a C# in the bass, making it a first inversion (see pages 48 and 49). Repeating a bass note (usually the root) against chord changes is a common feature of rock music and contributes to its expansive sound.

AC/DC make great use of space within the bar to increase anticipation. Their riffs should be played loudly, but often have a high melodic content—accurate damping with your fretting hand will help to avoid unwanted ringing strings.

 **TRACK 68**

EXERCISE II
Power-chord riff in D/C featuring an AC/DC-style first inversion of the A in the first bar.

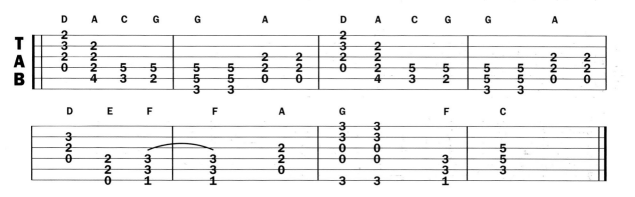

Van Halen–Style Riffs and Licks

When Van Halen released their eponymous debut album in 1978, it showcased nothing short of a reinvention of metal. Emphasizing teenage concerns and rock 'n' roll hedonism over the portentous and world weary, they brought flash, exuberance, and a shaft of L.A. sunshine back to heavy rock.

Guitarist Eddie Van Halen is the first-generation immigrant son of an accomplished Dutch bandleader, and there's no doubt that musical ability must run in the family. His arsenal of techniques includes two-handed tapping (see pages 132 and 133), harmonics (see pages 128 and 129), extreme tremolo "divebombs" (see page 59), and tremolo picking (fast, machine-gunlike picking that can help to sustain a note when harmony requires it), along with fast, graceful sweep picking.

He is no slouch in the rhythm-guitar department either, originating imaginative riffs that can be underplayed or overplayed (played with a greater or lesser number of notes and harder or softer picking), whichever is demanded by the vocal part. Exercise I features a riff like this, in A, that makes use of a classic metal-style A pedal

SETTING THE TONE

GAIN   BASS   MIDDLE   TREBLE   VOLUME

Eddie Van Halen favors Strat-shape guitars with locking tremolos and often plays with a humbucker at the bridge. He uses phasing mixed with a bypass signal and prefers EQ (equalization) with a scooped midrange.

note (see pages 42 and 43). The sustaining open G in the second bar could be muted or left to ring, and the whole part more or less damped with your picking hand,

TRACK 69

EXERCISE I
Quarter-tone bends against the tonic put this riff firmly in classic-rock territory. Continuing the A bass pedal against the Dadd4 (the subdominant) creates spacious harmonic ambiguity.

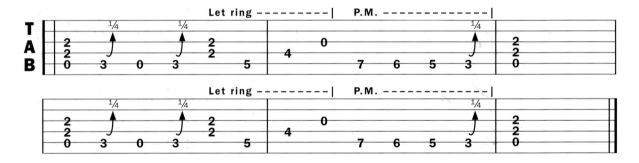

Eddie Van Halen
In 1978, the release of Van Halen's debut album, *Van Halen*, rewrote the rules for hard rock. Guitarist Eddie Van Halen had developed a lightning-fast technique, which incorporated a variety of two-handed tapping, hammer-ons, pull-offs, and effects. Original, inventive, and extreme, Van Halen went on to become the most popular American rock 'n' roll band of the late 1970s and early '80s, setting the bar high for hard rock and heavy metal that followed.

depending on whether your vocalist is letting rip with a lungful of passion or just looking pretty.

Exercise II features second-inversion major chords. Having the fifth in the bass, they are simply fretted in the case of barre chords with an A-string root, as they can be formed with a simple barre across the D, G, and B strings. Like the AC/DC-style riff on page 139, this is a good example of how metal players often use power chords to lead a melody. This riff has the sleazy, big-city feel heard on tracks such as "Running with the Devil."

TRACK 70

EXERCISE II
These second inversions create a strong Mixolydian feel against a sustained root E bass note.

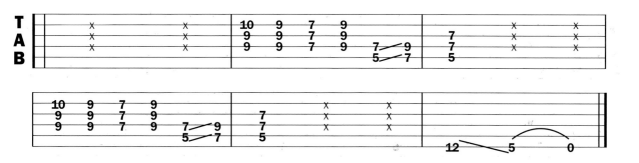

Metallica-Style Riffs

In the first half of the 1980s, Metallica helped to define the emerging genre of thrash metal, welding the riffing of Black Sabbath to the tempo of punk. Responding to commercial success, they then took their music in a more mainstream direction with 1986's *Master of Puppets*, featuring slower tempos and showcasing the band's more balladic side.

Metallica made early use of pickups specifically for metal players, with darker tones and the ability to produce more harmonic overtones than the classic older designs. Harmonics (see page 128) are a big feature of Kirk Hammett's solos, which usually feature sweep-picked arpeggios of pentatonic, blues, and whole- and half-tone scales (see pages 60 and 64). The band pioneered the modern metal sound of scooping, or cutting, mid-range frequencies, making for a sweet tone at saturated gain, with plenty of treble for harmonics.

Exercise I features a two-bar riff in E that would sit well in the verse of a Metallica track. Try playing it completely with downstrokes for added urgency. A power

chord built on the tritone (B♭) of the root scale (E) follows the E pedal note in the first bar, which builds anticipation, while the rest of the second bar consists of easy but effective diad power-chord fifths, facilitating fast, thrash-style changes.

Exercise II is an example of an open-string riff. Balladic in style, it should be played cleanly (i.e., undistorted), perhaps with a dash of chorus, for its lush modulating sound that can help to sustain the ringing E and B open strings. It consists of chord fragments in E major, ending in the dominant to imply its beginning again. Note how the final Bsus4 reinforces this since the fourth of the dominant is the root note of the tonic chord.

 **TRACK 71**

EXERCISE I

The blues-scale-based power-chord sequence in the second bar harmonizes a B♭5–B5–G5–F#5 progression.

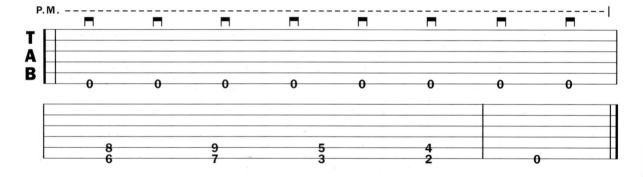

Kirk Hammett

Metallica's early releases included fast tempos, instrumentals, and aggressive musicianship that placed them as one of the "big four" of thrash metal—alongside Slayer, Megadeth, and Anthrax. Guitarist Hammett's influence helped create a more melodic and controlled sound and, always learning and improving, Hammett took lessons from Joe Satriani to broaden his style. From Satch he learned the techniques and intricacies of jazz, blues, and classical styles, and throughout the 1990s Hammet's playing shifted from his early metal roots to a more earthy, Hendrix-esque style.

SETTING THE TONE

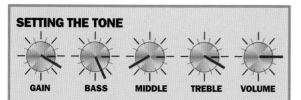

GAIN　　BASS　　MIDDLE　　TREBLE　　VOLUME

Kirk Hammett makes extensive use of a wah pedal, sometimes leaving it set in position as a tone-shaping device, like Michael Schenker. "The wah-wah is an extension of my personality…They'll have to cut off my leg if they want me to stop using the wah-wah pedal," he says.

 **TRACK 72**

EXERCISE II

Open E and B strings lend themselves to alternate picking in which the first two notes of each bar are picked with upstrokes and the second two with downstrokes.

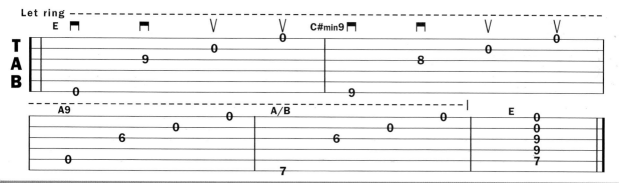

Slayer-Style Riffs

Thrash, black metal, death metal . . . arguments persist over the correct name for the genre. But whatever you call the speed-metal style, with practice, its techniques are easier to learn than they sound. Thanks to bands such as Megadeth, Pantera, and Lamb of God, together with genre pioneers Venom and Bathory, black metal has manifested itself in churning riffs, dark harmonies, and apocalyptic imagery for over thirty years.

Slayer's *Reign in Blood* album of 1986 (together with its near-title track, "Raining Blood"), is a benchmark of speed-metal techniques. Guitarists Kerry King and Jeff Hanneman trade ferocious licks, often in drop minor third tuning (see pages 134 and 135), and double lead parts fit to summon dark forces. If you want to make music that sounds like it's been dragged through a dungeon rather than a studio, arm yourself with the following aural torture techniques.

Exercise I, in D, demonstrates the speed-metal rhythm that's commonly known as "the gallop." To hear it is to know it. Play precisely with a firm picking technique. While accurate, coordinated fretting is

vital, this is really a workout for the picking hand. Play it with palm muting and without. Begin slowly and build up the tempo as you internalize the technique. Poor

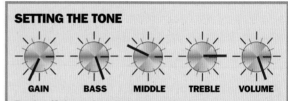

SETTING THE TONE

GAIN BASS MIDDLE TREBLE VOLUME

Back off the gain a little more than you may expect. While keeping your tone thick and saturated, it's important to give some definition to each note.

TRACK 73

EXERCISE I

A sixteenth-beat picking pattern is used for a D5–G5–C5 progression followed by a first inversion of G in bar four.

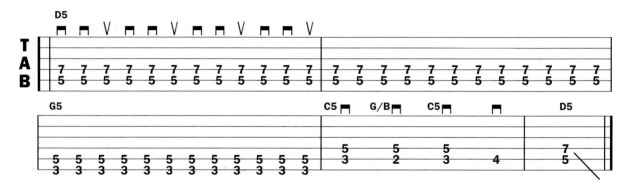

Kerry King
Apocalyptic in style and content, Slayer's King demonstrates doom-laden dexterity.

examples abound—it is not theory-laden, so only technique and practice stand between the good and the weak. Slayer tracks often contain a series of sections with differing rhythms and time signatures. Punky, upbeat 2/4 passages and plangent sections with a compound time signature (see pages 26 and 27)—requiring different picking speeds—may appear in the same song. Keeping your fretting hand rigid is—exceptionally—to be encouraged when it comes to accurate fretting of fast Slayer-style power chords with your first and third fingers.

King and Hanneman play riffs with the doom-laden intervals of Tony Iommi and the dexterity of Eddie Van Halen. Exercise II features an E-minor riff that could be Slayer's thanks to the twisted use of intervals such as the flat fifth (B♭). Once you have mastered it, play against a recording or loop of the riff, at the same frets, one string higher for each note. This will give you a perfect fourth parallel harmony—an instantly recognizable metal sound.

TRACK 74

EXERCISE II

This riff requires a precise picking technique. Letting the low E ring adds to the sense of menace.

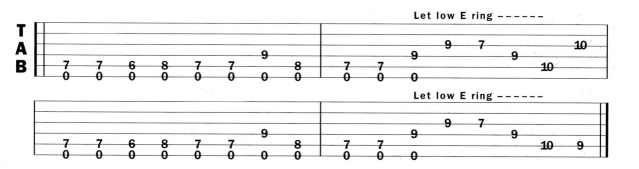

Classic Slash-Style Licks

The chart-storming popularity of Guns N' Roses' breakthrough album, *Appetite for Destruction*, made the metal world sit up and take notice of the band when it was released in 1987. Critically dismissed as sleazy rock 'n' rollers amidst the squeaky-clean, poodle-haired glam-metal acts that populated L.A. at that time, GNR showed that super-fast solos and sophisticated, multi-tracked overdubbing were no match for classic rock riffs, songs sung from the heart, and simple but effective licks where the wider record-buying public was concerned.

Slash reinterpreted classic "feel"-based guitar playing for a new generation of suburban kids the world over, becoming one of the most recognizable musicians in the world thanks to his trademark top hat, long hair, and shades, together with his appearance in the phenomenally successful game *Guitar Hero III* (all the time obscuring his actual features—clever man!).

As Guns N' Roses eventually foundered in a morass of recording perfectionism, Slash continued to purvey his brand of storming blues-based rock with Velvet Revolver and by working as a sideman and songwriter

"WOMAN TONE"
With few effects between guitar and amp (besides wah), Slash's sound is an updated version of Clapton's classic Les Paul "woman tone," achieved with the neck pickup volume full up, the bridge somewhere around five or six, and both tone controls down, with the selector in the out-of-phase (middle) position. However, opinion is divided, and some guitarists maintain it requires the neck pickup only.

 **TRACK 75**

EXERCISE I
Add smooth, saturated distortion and this intricate legato figure is instant Slash!

for the world's biggest recording artists, such as Michael Jackson.

Exercise I features an approximation of a sweet Slash-style riff for you to make your own. This evocative lick uses an eight-bar cycle in F with the two chords that punctuate the arpeggios alternating every four.

Exercise II is based on another Slash favorite—the minor blues scale played against a fast-riffing rhythm part, in this case a I–V–IV–I progression in F#, with a chromatic bass run featuring both the minor and major seventh. The lead part features classic unison bends to the F# octave and hammer-ons together with the minor third against the dominant for a firm blues flavor.

 **TRACK 76**

Slash

Slick and super-fast, Slash favors vibrato and hammer-ons and pull-offs to create speed. His picking hand isn't used for speed; instead he uses it to add a percussive feel to his solos. His style is based around the blues and harmonic minor scales, and he plays with a strong, melodic feel.

EXERCISE II

F# minor blues scale licks and bends embellished with Slash-style wah.

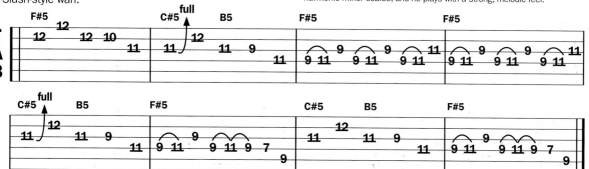

Your First Heavy Metal
Song with Solo

Many of the great tracks that came out of metal's second wave in the late 1980s, such as Rainbow's "Since You've Been Gone," sound like classic hard rock tracks now. This is because other metal bands of the time—including Motörhead, Iron Maiden, and Judas Priest—set the tone for the genre's direction. Dropped tunings, sweep-picked shred-style solos, and lyrics based on myths or historic battles became the norm.

TRACK 77

The following track consists of a verse part that couldn't be more sick! First of all, the guitar is detuned by a whole tone. Secondly, the verse progression moves from a power-chord tonic to a power-chord minor third, and from the tonic once more to the flat fifth (tritone). Oh, and thirdly, it's in 5/4 time, so you will need to count five beats to the bar.

With your bottom string detuned a further tone (so it in effect becomes "drop-C" tuning), you could play this riff entirely on the bottom two strings (see pages 130 and 131). Our chords follow a menacing, no-nonsense D–F–D–G# progression, and the tabbed part alternates between open and damped playing, featuring palm muting such as might back a metal vocalist's subterranean growl.

The chorus oscillates between power chords built on the dominant and the augmented fifth (see page 117), together with the subdominant. The solo, featuring tremolo-picked chromatic runs, together with the sixteenth-beat double-bass-drum pattern, nod darkly at today's lords of black metal.

Dave Murray
Iron Maiden was one of the late seventies' English heavy metal bands boasting simple guitar riffs, shrieking vocals, and bone-crunching chords. Their work has inspired other sub-genres of heavy metal music, including power metal and speed metal. Guitarist Murray's style is mainly legato-based solos, and he is noted for having naturally strong fingers—all the better for his frequent use of hammer-ons and pull-offs.

VERSE

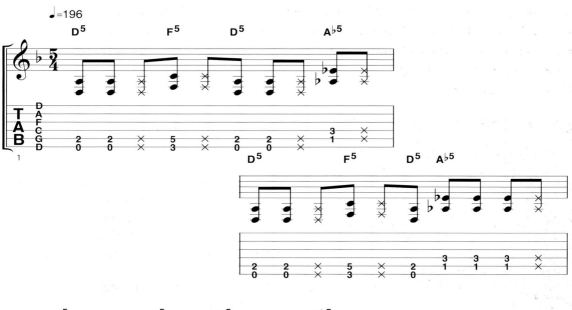

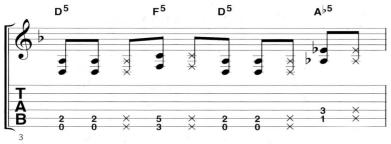

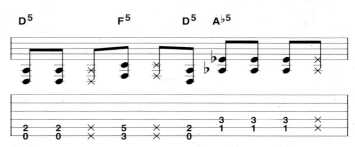

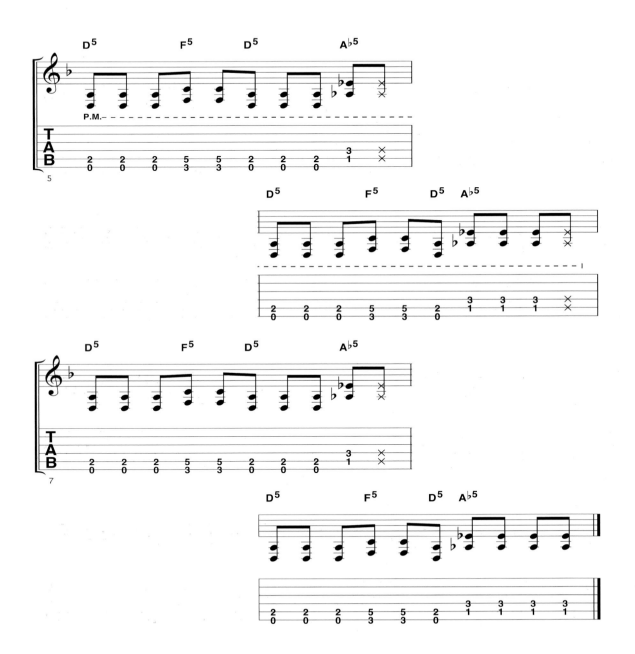

CHORUS

SOLO

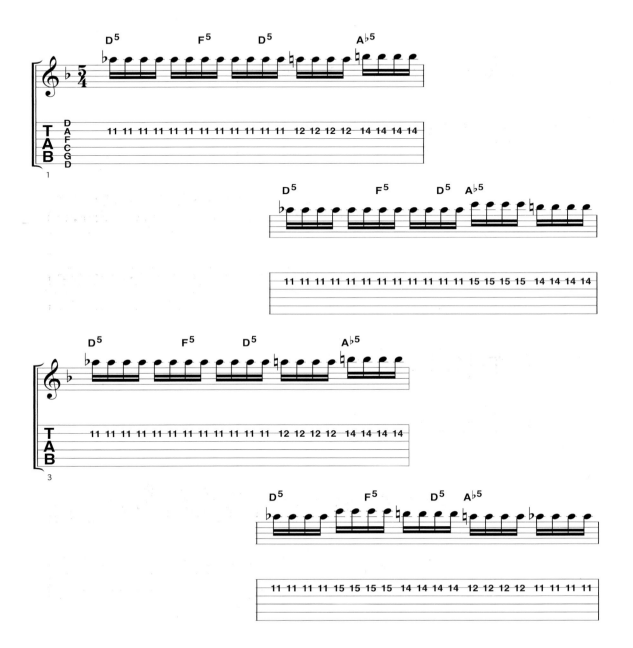

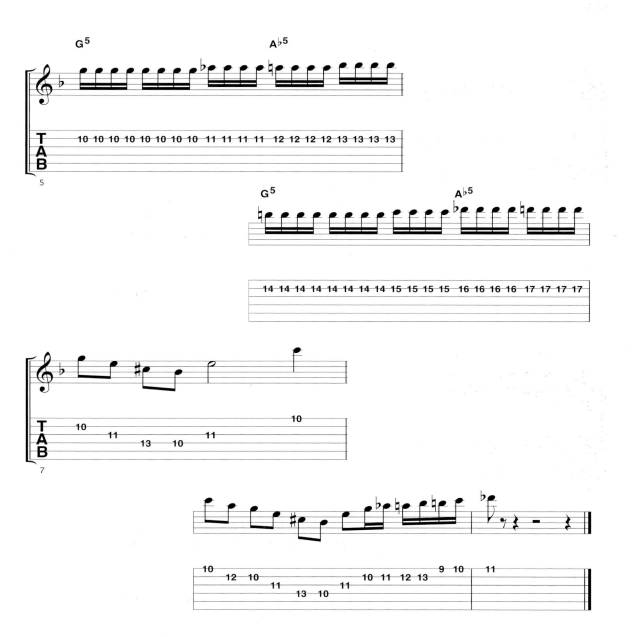

Play Rhythm Guitar

Don't be fooled into thinking that lead guitar parts hold all of the interest in a piece of music—those fragments of melody would not have the impact they do without the harmony established behind them. Rhythm guitar is the backbone of rock. Without it, you've got no riffs, no groove, and no song! It doesn't matter how good your solos are, if you can't lay down a cool groove, nobody's going to play with you. And don't assume your rhythm part must be limited to strumming or arpeggiating standard voicings of chords. Develop your understanding of intervals and use this musical freedom to get away from the standard chord shapes as much as possible.

Maybe yours is the only guitar in the band, and you are already thinking about the techniques and phrases that will fill out the harmonic space left by the bass and drums most effectively. But, if you have two or more in your lineup, think about how both guitars can be doing something harmonically interesting at all times, without crowding each other—strumming barre chords is a wasted opportunity. When playing rhythm parts, the guitar is acting as part of the rhythm section. So think in terms of "locking in" with the drummer and bass player. Like a drummer, you are looking to develop pin-sharp, "on the beat" hand coordination.

Fender Telecaster
The Telecaster is known for producing both bright, cutting tones or mellow, warm, bluesy tones, depending on which pickup is selected—"bridge" pickup for the former, "neck" pickup the latter. This makes it a hugely versatile guitar, good for most styles of music, from blues to rock to jazz.

Using Chord Extensions
to Create Color

In addition to the open and barre chord shapes featured on pages 24, 25, 30, and 31, there's a wealth of extended chords—with notes added by stacking one or more thirds above the basic four-note seventh chord—available to you, used either to integrate melody into a chord progression or to come up with a complex and interesting harmonic structure.

Solid rhythm playing requires not just a great strumming arm but a knowledge of chords that incorporate these "color" notes. Jazz and swing guitarists are often required to change chord on every beat! The influence of jazz on the blues has resulted in fusion styles in which progressions of very complex chords can be seamlessly shoehorned into simple twelve-bar progressions.

Neither are extended or color chords the preserve of jazz-fusion. Great funk rhythm players such as Curtis Mayfield often feature extended chords in alternative tunings. Extended chords feature hugely in the melodic pop of the 1990s and in indie and alternative rock bands of the 2000s. The sounds of major sevenths and ninths are now as familiar to us as simple majors and minors.

The major seventh is one such example. The following exercises use the chord shapes from pages 188 and 189 and are designed to familiarize you with certain sounds and how they can be used. We can only cover the most popular sounds from the panoply of possible altered-chord voicings, but with the scalar knowledge gained from pages 22, 23, 110, and 111, you should be able to identify them when they occur, based on the intervals from a scale that have been added to the chord.

Major sevenths have a warm, static sound compared to the dominant seventh (see pages 30 and 31). This should be audible in the second half of Exercise I. Exercise II features the C minor natural seventh and the C minor sixth, which are altered to contain the melodic cadence.

TRACK 78/1

EXERCISE I

A D minor ninth dominant chord resolves neatly to a tonic (G) seventh.

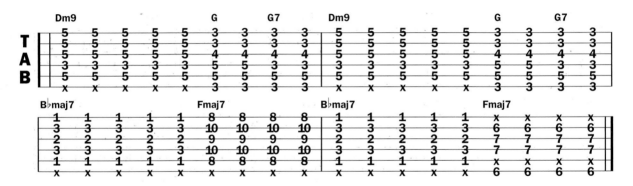

Curtis Mayfield
Innovative, soulful, and too often overlooked, Curtis Mayfield was a pioneer of 1970s funk and helped to introduce urban commentary into soul music, adding rhythms that became the trademark flourishes of Chicago soul. His 1972 soundtrack, *Superfly,* was a landmark recording, with its uplifting melodies and fabulous funk-pop arrangements.

Secondary dominants, meanwhile, can be added to a progression without changing its key, so they are great for creating interest behind the major blues scale. They are non-diatonic dominant seventh chords—for any chords other than diminished, you can play a seventh chord (a natural—dominant, as opposed to major—seventh, with a major third) based on its fifth. These are chord substitutions rather than extensions.

The possible combinations of extended chords are infinite. But one should not miss out on suspended fourths, or "sus-4s"—"suspended," because the third is absent from the chord, strengthening the sound. Moving from a fourth to its major chord creates instant tension and resolution—recognizable from the impactful opening bars of The Who's "Pinball Wizard."

 TRACK 78/2

EXERCISE II

The C minor seventh chord that begins this progression is a second inversion, with the flat fifth as its lowest note.

```
      Cm7                           Cm6                         Cm7                           Cm6
    | x    x    x    x    x    x    x    x    x  | x    x    x    x    x    x    x    x    x  |
T   | 10   10   10   10   10   10   10   10   10 | 10   10   10   10   10   10   10   10   10 |
A   | 9    9    9    9    9    8    8    8    8  | 9    9    9    9    9    8    8    8    8  |
B   | 10   10   10   10   10   10   10   10   10 | 10   10   10   10   10   10   10   10   10 |
    | 9    9    9    9    9    9    9    9    9  | 9    9    9    9    9    9    9    9    9  |
    | x    x    x    x    x    x    x    x    x  | x    x    x    x    x    x    x    x    x  |

      Cm7                           Cm6                         Fdim                  A              A7
    | x    x    x    x    x    x    x    x    x  | x    x    x    x    x  | 5    5    5    5    5    5  |
    | 10   10   10   10   10   10   10   10   10 | 9    9    9    9    9    5    5    5    5    8    8  |
    | 9    9    9    9    9    8    8    8    8  | 7    7    7    7    6    6    6    6    6    6    6  |
    | 10   10   10   10   10   10   10   10   10 | 9    9    9    9    9    7    7    7    7    7    7  |
    | 9    9    9    9    9    9    9    9    9  | 8    8    8    8    8    0    0    0    0    0    0  |
    | x    x    x    x    x    x    x    x    x  | x    x    x    x    x    x    x    x    x    x    x  |
```

Jimi Hendrix–Style Chords

Jimi Hendrix set fire to his guitar, played it behind his head, and even picked the strings with his teeth. The consummate showman also created new and exciting sounds that revolutionized rock music. His career was meteoric and short-lived, but his work is a legacy that still inspires and influences players to this day.

No overnight success, he spent years as a "sideman" and guitarist with touring blues and soul acts such as The Isley Brothers before Chas Chandler brought him to the UK. There he honed the chord voicings he would use in his own songwriting. The shows were stomping soul reviews designed to get feet tapping and hands clapping in theaters such as Harlem's Apollo, and Hendrix's style was influenced by the driving snare drums and "stabbing" rhythmic style of soul's brass sections. His legacy stands at an axis between the blues and soul that influenced him and the rock and metal that he would influence.

He had in mind to use his guitar to emulate the parts of a big band as much as possible, and to wring the maximum effect from single lines and simple intervals. A touring musician without much to his name, the young Hendrix thought about how he could turn a guitar into his own orchestra—hence Hendrix's music is typified by a vast sound with often surprisingly few notes involved.

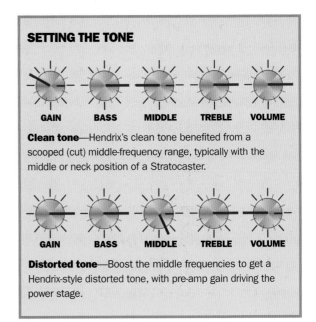

SETTING THE TONE

GAIN   BASS   MIDDLE   TREBLE   VOLUME

Clean tone—Hendrix's clean tone benefited from a scooped (cut) middle-frequency range, typically with the middle or neck position of a Stratocaster.

GAIN   BASS   MIDDLE   TREBLE   VOLUME

Distorted tone—Boost the middle frequencies to get a Hendrix-style distorted tone, with pre-amp gain driving the power stage.

TRACK 79/1

JIMI'S FIFTHS

Hendrix used a simple, widely spaced fifth voicing that is more mellow than the traditional power-chord V (see page 44) but which covers a vast tonal range. It's great to use up and down the neck, provided you damp the strings above your index and third fingers. The wide, spacey feel of "Love or Confusion" derives from this chord, shown here in G:

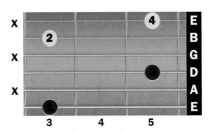

Jimi Hendrix

A master at drawing all sorts of previously unheard sounds from his instrument, often with novel amplification experiments that produced awesome feedback and roaring distortion, Jimi Hendrix expanded the vocabulary of the electric rock guitar more than anyone before or since. His virtuoso guitar playing employed an array of musical adornments, including wah-wah, buzzing feedback, distorted riffs, and super-fast, fluid runs up and down the scales. Often called the greatest electric guitarist in the history of rock music by other musicians, and one of the most important musicians of his era, *Rolling Stone* named Hendrix the top guitarist on its list of the "100 Greatest Guitarists of All Time."

> **"Sometimes you want to give up the guitar, you'll hate the guitar. But if you stick with it, you're gonna be rewarded."**
>
> *Jimi Hendrix*

TRACK 79/2

DOMINANT SEVENTH SHARP NINTH

The dominant seventh sharp ninth is so associated with him that many musicians simply refer to it as "the Hendrix chord." Hear it in "Purple Haze" and implied throughout "Foxy Lady." It has elements of major and minor, consisting of: I, III, V, minor VII, #9—in G: G, B, D, F, A sharp; in E: E, A♭, D, G. His traditional voicing of it is strengthened by the two extra open strings featuring the tonic. Shown here in E:

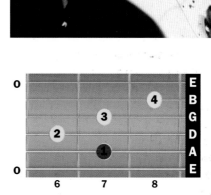

TRACK 79/3

MAJOR THIRD IN D

Hendrix used a voicing that can be substituted wherever a major chord is in use, such as the first, fourth, and fifth chords of the key. Mellow but with an interesting color, Hendrix uses it in songs that sound like he's explaining something to us, such as "Castles Made of Sand." It has the advantage, too, of allowing you to hammer-on to the third from the second, two frets below on the A string, as Hendrix does in "The Wind Cries Mary."

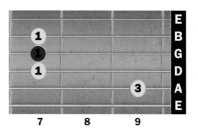

Rolling Stones–Style Rhythm Sound

It's incredible to think that The Rolling Stones will soon be celebrating a half century of nonstop rock 'n' roll. Beginning as a rhythm and blues band in the early 1960s, they were among the first to popularize African-American music in Europe, and re-exported it to its home country. Following the success of "(I Can't Get No) Satisfaction" in 1965, with its simple, iconic riff, the Stones went on to explore more melodic territory through a series of classic rock albums that used folk tunings to allow and inspire altered-chord and color-note progressions that aren't possible in conventional tuning.

Keith Richards was not originally a fan of "Satisfaction," at least in the form it was released. Rumor has it that, in working on the song, he had felt it too close to "Dancing in the Street" by Martha and the Vandellas. Laying down a guide part for a Stax-style horn section, he added the fuzz to better represent the fluidity of brass instruments; he was outvoted at a subsequent management meeting in which the decision was taken to release that version as the single.

Exercise I superimposes a triad a fourth above the root. This creates the second inversions (with the fifth in the bass) of the C and F.

TRACK 80

OPEN-G TUNING

After drop-D tuning, open-G is perhaps the most common rock tuning, and easily achieved. Simply tune to an open G-major chord (see pages 24–25):

Strings:
  1-D   2-B   3-D   4-G   5-B   6-G

You'll notice that there is no change to standard tuning on the second, third, and fourth strings. Adding color notes such as the fourth and major second, as in Exercise II, becomes much easier, as you can now make a major barre chord with your index finger. In this tuning, Keith Richards removes his bottom (sixth) D string.

EXERCISE I

Open-G tuning allows you to create punchy riffs with one movable chord shape.

```
            C/G                              G                    C
T                                                                 5
A        13                13              12                     5
B        12                12              12                     5
         14                14              12                     5
         12                12              12                     5

            F/C       C     F/C       C     F/C       C           C
         5        5     5       5      5        5      5          5
         5        6     5       6      5        6      5          5
         5        5     5       5      5        5      5          5
         5        7     5       7      5        7      5          5
         5        5     5       5      5        5      5          5
```

The Beatles and The Stones

During their active recording careers, these two musical titans were often contrasted in the press, which loved the imagined "boy next door" versus "bad boy" narrative it wove around the bands. The two bands were interestingly different in musical terms, however: George Harrison remains an underrated lead guitarist—his crisp, clean, precise arrangements brought cohesion to the different songwriting styles of Lennon and McCartney. Where the Stones borrowed from the blues and developed its progressions for their own songs, the Beatles were a kick-ass rock 'n' roll band who subsequently went on to develop pop and to take imaginative harmonic liberties. They rewrote the rulebook for melodic pop—as opposed to rock—songwriting, a legacy heard daily in the music of today's good-looking boy and girl bands.

Keith Richards

Keith Richards's blues-style, chunky guitar riffs that so dominated the Stones's hits such as "(I Can't Get No) Satisfaction," "Jumpin' Jack Flash," and "Honky-Tonk Woman," have led him to be considered as one of the greatest rhythm guitarists in rock 'n' roll, and arguably the finest blues-based rhythm guitarist in the genre. Like his idol, Chuck Berry, Richards has created some of the most memorable riffs in rock. Preferring open-chord tunings drawn from Delta blues, Richard's guitars were often strung with five strings for clean fingering, which accentuated his distinctive sound.

Exercise II, meanwhile, features shuffle licks (see page 76) that include simultaneous fourths and sixths. Marrying Richards's Chuck Berry influence (see pages 100 to 101) to the possibilities of open G, these were used to great effect throughout the Stones's run of back-to-back classic albums in the late 1960s and early 1970s.

 **TRACK 81**

EXERCISE II

A two-bar chord-based riff typically used as a verse accompaniment.

161

The Red Hot Chili Peppers–
Style Riffs

Formed in 1983, L.A.'s The Red Hot Chili Peppers have proved themselves capable of mixing super-cool funk grooves as authentic and exciting as any from the 1970s with melodic and meaningful songwriting and a reflective, bluesy twist. They have endured a variety of lineup changes to re-emerge every time as a thrilling live act, unpretentious yet able to hold the attention of a festival-sized audience with nothing more than a basic single-guitar lineup (augmented by a second guitarist on their "Stadium Arcadium" tour).

Perhaps more than any other contemporary band, they've made it their business to pursue—and capture—the elusive improvisational chemistry that makes a group of musicians more than the sum of its parts. Guitarist John Frusciante has superb taste, channelling Hendrix, Parliament Funkadelic, and The Ohio Players, 1980s rap and punk, and art rockers like Television's Tom Verlaine. Frusciante writes licks, riffs, and chord sequences that have managed to retain the loyalty of their funk rock fans while broadening their appeal with more conventional balladry.

The band's first funk-rock (or rap-rock) phase culminated in the album *Blood Sugar Sex Magik*. Playing in this style involves sticking to a groove—it's not unusual to have one-chord verses, for example, with interest deriving from the riff. Exercise I is edgy, funk-friendly, and written to maintain a groove in which a syncopated, fingerstyle bass line would lead the melody.

This is a workout for the strumming hand. You are looking to maintain metronomic timing. The second your hand stops moving, you will have lost the groove! To this end, practice "ghost" or "phantom" strumming (which couldn't be less spooky): maintain your strumming action even when your pick is not in contact with the strings (as indicated in bars two and four). You'll see how this style lends itself to on-the-beat changes of altered chords,

TRACK 82

EXERCISE I

E-based funk-rock riff to which the Em9 in bars two and four adds color.

SETTING THE TONE

| GAIN | BASS | MIDDLE | TREBLE | VOLUME |

Frusciante generally plays clean enough that every note can be heard, eschewing the saturated distortion that RHCP guitarists Hilel Slovak and Dave Navarro used. Subtle use of compression, chorus, and overdrive help him to switch between funk and rock tones.

such as the sevenths and ninths commonly used in funk rhythm style.

Frusciante's playing, especially on the album *Californication*, can be melodic and abrasive even within the same song, featuring classic Hendrix-style chord sequences which are concise and not done to death, in line with the band's punk influence. Exercise II, in A, features a typical minor-pentatonic lick that can be repeated as a groove lick or used singly as a verse fill, or as a lead-in to a melodic chorus consisting of harmonized chords.

John Frusciante
Former guitarist of the rock/funk band Red Hot Chili Peppers, Frusciante's music always seems to be evolving. Influenced by guitarists of various genres, Frusciante's playing emphasizes melody, and he has developed what he calls a "grimy" sound—using lots of distortion in his solos.

 TRACK 83

EXERCISE II

Funky single-note riff in A. This requires a precise combination of picking and fretting-hand damping.

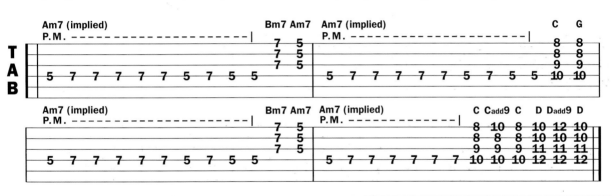

Foo Fighters–Style Rhythms and Riffs

Following the sudden, sorry end of Nirvana in 1994 (see pages 178 and 179), drummer Dave Grohl's career took a redemptive turn with new band the Foo Fighters. Their subsequent multiple Grammy Award–winning success has probably proved as surprising to Grohl himself as to anyone, coming as unexpectedly as a sighting of one of their namesakes—"foo fighter" being military code for a UFO.

Foo Fighters gigs are stadium fillers. Their popularity is attributed not just to Grohl's down-to-earth character but to his way with a riff. He has a drummer's sense of rhythm guitar playing, with more changes of time signature than the typical band of the post-punk era. Once a prog-rock preserve, complex timing changes, in the Foo Fighters's hands, are made to sound concise and easy to digest.

Grohl, as the band's chief songwriter, is also not afraid to vary the number of bars in song sections to include odd numbers—very unusual in rock and all the more so for their seamless inclusion. The chorus of "Times Like These," for example, repeats in cycles of three bars.

Exercise I features the kind of power-chord riff that could sound massive in their hands, thanks to its harmonic ambiguity. The band dispenses with extended

solos in favor of melodic hooks of the kind found in Exercise II, just one of the ways in which they marry rock and pop styles—perhaps the single biggest factor in their broad fan base.

SETTING THE TONE

GAIN   BASS   MIDDLE   TREBLE   VOLUME

Dave Grohl and fellow Foo Fighter guitarist Chris Shiflett use cleaner sounds than you might expect, with classic, overdriven—"British"– or "tweed"– style—amp tones.

 TRACK 84

EXERCISE I

Alternate picking, together with counting the bar as "1–2–3–1–2–3–4," will help you into the groove of this harmonically ambiguous riff in D.

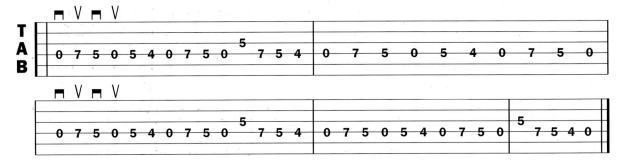

> **"I love Black Sabbath. They made an amazing contribution to music today. Almost every band that made it big in the 1990s owes a debt to them."**
>
> *Dave Grohl* (Foo Fighters)

Dave Grohl

When Grohl first started the Foo Fighters, after Nirvana disbanded following Kurt Cobain's death, the Foo Fighters's music was often compared to Nirvana's. Like the Pixies and Nirvana, Foo Fighters's songs shift between quiet verses and loud choruses, a technique that Grohl puts down to the fact that the members of Nirvana liked bands such as the Beatles and ABBA as much as Flipper and Black Flag. His eclectic musical tastes and hugely rhythmic riffs make Grohl's songwriting unique and refreshing. The forward momentum of his musical approach led Grohl to state in 2005, "I love being in a rock band, but I don't know if I necessarily wanna be in an alternative rock band from the 1990s for the rest of my life."

 TRACK 85

EXERCISE II

Chromatic-style riff in E that's a Foo Fighters's combination of lead and rhythm parts.

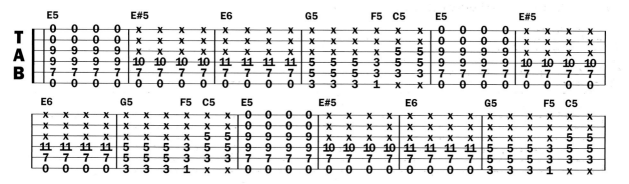

165

Your First
Rhythm Song

Our rhythm song follows a I–V–IV progression in G. Like all the tunes featured at the ends of these chapters, it provides you with three parts, breaking down the constituent elements of the vast majority of classic rock and pop songs—which consist of the tried-and-tested "verse–chorus–verse–chorus–break– verse–chorus" formula.

Common variations include beginning with a chorus, if not a separate introductory passage, or ending with a double chorus. Breaks—which, when well-executed, occur before the listener's tired of hearing the main progression—might over- or underplay the main refrain, or introduce a whole other chord sequence (often based on the relative minor of a song's tonal center—see page 33).

Playing the jangling G5 chord that begins the refrain with a downstroke will help you pick the cadence in time, alternately with the ringing open-D pedal note. The verse progression, meanwhile, shows how you can add interest to a simple progression (voiced here variously as full diatonic barre chords, octaves, and fifths): the second

part here could be an understated lead part, or the bass line. The point is that it lasts for four cycles of the verse progression (see page 174)—taking it somewhere different and adding interest each time it does.

The chorus part, meanwhile, (which might equally function as a break) begins with the V and features a ringing "add4" voicing of the dominant, D, that benefits from alternate sixteenth-beat picking. (This is not a "sus4" because the third—the absence of which makes such a chord a suspended chord—is still present.)

 TRACK 86

Graham Coxon
Considered one of Britain's most inventive and eclectic guitar heroes, Graham Coxon is perhaps still best known as guitarist of the Britpop alt rock band Blur. Having arranged some of the band's most exquisite music, Coxon also helped to popularize the Britpop genre. Blur, influenced by English guitar pop groups such as The Kinks, the Beatles, and XTC, released such classic Britpop albums as *Modern Life Is Rubbish* (1993), *Parklife* (1994), and *The Great Escape* (1995).

REFRAIN

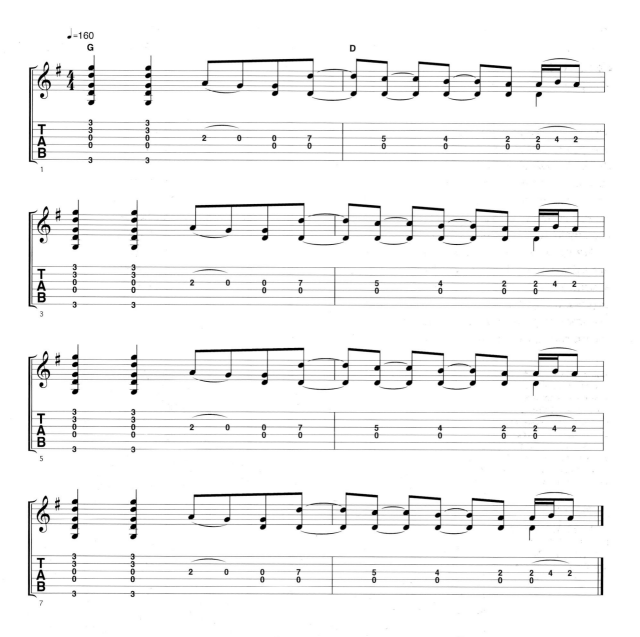

VERSE

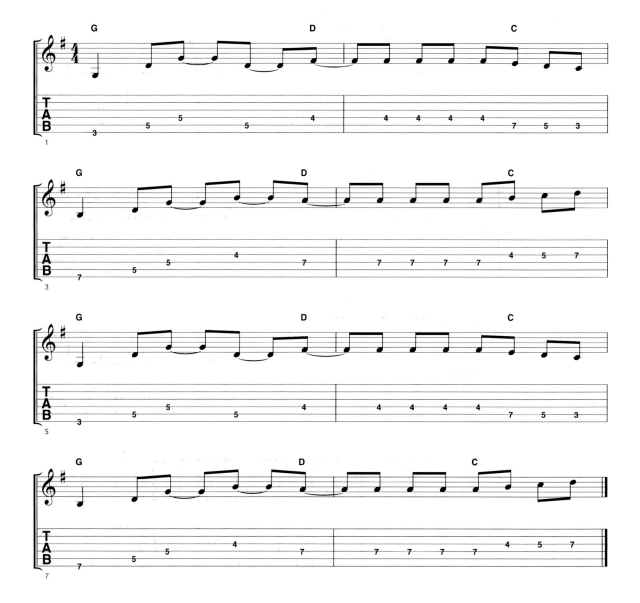

CHORUS

Play Alternative Rock

Television, The Smiths, the Pixies, Pavement—at first, the more famous alternative rock bands may not seem to have a lot in common. That's because the genre is perhaps best described as the playground for great ideas. Many ideas that have crossed into the mainstream have come from small scenes, often in student-dominated towns, where the gigs are small, the stakes are low, and musicians have enjoyed the freedom to experiment. Kurt Cobain, for example (see page 178), was the first to admit that the quiet, often damped verses of the Pixies's songs, which gave way to crashing, cathedral-like choruses, were a major influence on Nirvana tracks such as "Smells like Teen Spirit." The Velvet Underground, perhaps the greatest "alt rock" band of all time, wrote droning guitar parts to complement the sustained notes of John Cale's viola. Whether or not you're a fan of the bands, you may not think alternative rock has much to contribute for the would-be virtuoso rock guitarist. However, sometimes a little off-the-wall inventiveness can go a long way toward pleasing a crowd. The following chapter picks out a few of the most rocking techniques.

Fender Jaguar
The Jaguar's overall sound is more aggressive but thinner than Fender's other "Offset Waist Contour Body" guitar, the Jazzmaster. The tremolo/bridge design and the pickups produce a percussive sound, and playing the bridge pickup alone with the "strangle" switch—so called, apparently, because it cuts through all other band sounds—adds an icy, sharp tone.

Barre Chords and
Punk-Style Riffs

By the mid-1970s, the concise, to-the-point riffing of the great blues rock bands had given way to repetitious ten-minute solos. Young music fans decided to return to the first principles of rock 'n' roll, making music that addressed the lives and problems of teenagers in the way that Chuck Berry or Eddie Cochran songs do.

TRACK 87

EXERCISE I
Simple three-chord punk riff requiring accurate fretting-hand damping.

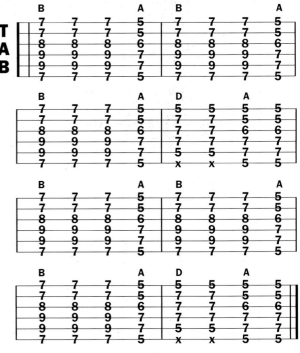

Mick Jones
Lead guitarist and vocalist for the Clash, one of the most exciting and explosive bands in rock 'n' roll history, Mick Jones played a major role in the birth and life of punk with his up-tempo punk-rock sound.

Punks therefore brought chords back to the front of the mix—often the same chord progressions that in classic or blues-rock might form the basis for a series of riffs and licks. Often played at breakneck tempos, their interest comes from the sheer energy and brio with which you play them.

TRACK 88

EXERCISE II

Punk bands often displayed a deceptively evolved sense of harmony, relying on chords for melody but using a lot of chords. This progression adds chords in C to the third classic-rock exercise on page 113, coming up with a potential chorus part.

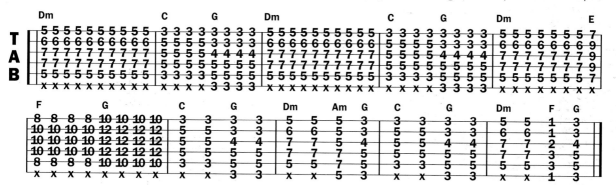

TRACK 89

EXERCISE III

Punk lead lines are often concise, quirky, and angular, such as this double-stop riff in B that uses notes from the underlying chords.

Post-Punk
Techniques

Punks made up with imagination what they lacked in musicianship. Here are just three legacies of the new wave era.

For many guitarists, delay is their next best friend after distortion or overdrive, used for sounds from atmospheric rock solos like David Gilmour's to rockabilly slapback echo. The post-punk years saw delay pioneered as a more rhythmic effect, as musicians found ways to push the limitations of punk.

Delay: The first requirement of using delay effectively in a band context is having a good relationship with your drummer. They must be able to (swallow a degree of ego and) play off the beat set by your delay time, rather than setting the tempo in the way they are used to, and they must be able to hear you—monitoring is always a problem for drummers, and it could help to consult them on where you position your amp. For shorter analogue-style delay times, this is not so important.

The Edge popularized rhythmic delay, adding haunting and atmospheric sounds to U2's anthemic bombast. Before him, it was pioneered by Keith Levine from PIL and Magazine's John McGeogh. Most useful delay times are found between 200 and 800 milliseconds. This goes for Exercise I, depending on the tempo at which you try it, which uses delay to add a groove to minor arpeggios.

Cycles: The more artistic punk and post-punk bands such as Wire often added harmonic interest to otherwise repetitive chord changes by doubling the length of the riff or bass line that is played against them, and adding a whole new "answering" melody typically twice the number of bars of the rhythm riff, though the whole could be four times longer than a single rhythm riff, or even the entire length of a verse (see page 166).

 **TRACK 90/1**

EXERCISE I

Play this with a delay of around 350 milliseconds. Playing the D5 arpeggio against the A and G makes the A, Aadd4 and the G, Gadd9.

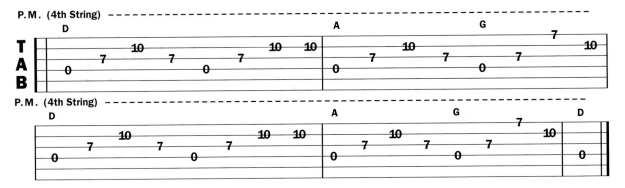

The Edge
The Edge has been crucial in defining U2's sound with his trademark low-key, percussive style of playing and distinctive chiming sound, achieved with extensive use of delay effects and reverb. He says, "I like a nice ringing sound on guitar, and most of my chords I find two strings and make them ring the same note, so it's almost like a 12-string sound."

Reggae and ska grooves: From deep, dreadlocked dub to up-tempo ska, West Indian sounds were UK chartbusters in the 1980s, and calypso-derived grooves have always lent themselves to narrative, reflective songwriting. They derive their fluidity from emphasizing the third beat of the bar. Listen to a reggae track and hear how the snare beat falls on the third beat of the bar: ///s///s///s///s/, as opposed to a conventional rock rhythm (whether "two-four" or "four-four" or its compounds): /s/s/s/s/s/s/s/s. The time signature doesn't change; it's a matter of emphasis.

Ska rhythms usually feature a deep, rounded bass and a bright, clean rhythm guitar. For any lead parts, think about what a horn section might do. Playing ska and reggae involves playing around that snare beat, on the second and fourth, and guitarists often find playing on the upstroke useful for establishing the rhythm. Exercise II features the kind of rhythm riff a punk or new wave band would have used to incorporate the groove into their set.

TRACK 90/2

EXERCISE II

Upstrokes on the second and fourth beats, together with barre chord voicings, lend a reggae flavor to these third and fifth diad arpeggios adapted from Exercise III on page 141.

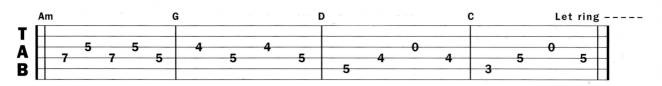

Johnny Marr's Sound

Johnny Marr blazed a trail of highly original guitar playing in the early to mid-1980s as guitarist and songwriting partner of The Smiths. Their music stood in contrast to the rock, metal, and post-punk of the era, with its power chords and fast, pentatonic-based solos, in having melodic, solo-free arrangements that used color notes (see pages 156 and 157) and unpredictable song structures to generate interest.

Marr favored Rickenbackers and Telecasters, their bright, jangly tones a perfect foil for unexpectedly funky and melody-leading bass lines, and made use of ninth and major seventh chords familiar from soul and jazz. These are often arpeggiated, however, rather than strummed, funk-style (see page 164 and 165), so it's no surprise that Marr claims inspiration from Neil Young and English folk, too.

Despite writing melodic, rather than blues-based progressions, he is very much a "feel" player, and no slouch with a bottleneck slide, either: "What I say, to all these potential songwriters, is that C to F or G to D is great. You can put a melody over it. Forget the idea of playing really fast scales or inverted chords, it's more

about feel." Marr's influence on the subsequent Manchester scene—from The Stone Roses's Jon Squire to Oasis's Noel Gallagher (who calls him "a f***ing wizard")—was immense, and The Smiths's album *The Queen Is Dead* regularly crops up near the top of those perennial, periodical "best album" polls.

Marr used tremolo and delay to great effect on tracks such as "How Soon Is Now," which borrows the classic Bo Diddley shuffle rhythm. He often tunes his guitar up a tone in standard tuning. Exercise I involves both fretted and open strings ringing together. In keeping with the best players in single-guitar bands, Marr's riffs often suggest the underlying chord progression, as here. Exercise II features two typical

TRACK 91

EXERCISE I
Ringing minor arpeggio riff that implies Dm/C/G. It may take a little practice to play so that the notes ring together.

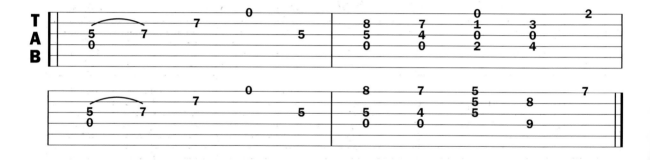

Johnny Marr
Marr's jangly funk-style guitar style became synonymous with The Smiths's sound, described by *Encyclopedia Britannica* as "non-rhythm-and-blues, whiter-than-white fusion of 1960s rock and post-punk was a repudiation of contemporary dance pop."

"BO DIDDLEY" RHYTHM

Bo Diddley was a barnstorming live performer, a contemporary and label mate of Chuck Berry, who popularized the gutsy shuffle rhythm that was often counted using the phrase, "shave and a haircut, six bits." It was borrowed by Buddy Holly for "Not Fade Away," by The Rolling Stones, and countless others. Diddley-inspired rhythms permeate popular music, such as in David Bowie's "Jean Genie," which uses the rhythm of Diddley's "Cops and Robbers." In keeping with their hypnotic beat, Diddley's songs often eschew the twelve-bar and stay on one chord for an entire verse.

Marr tricks—voicing ninths and major sevenths, and again using open, ringing strings against partial chord voicings to increase the chiming tone.

TRACK 92

SETTING THE TONE

| GAIN | BASS | MIDDLE | TREBLE | VOLUME |

Johnny Marr goes for a clean, bell-like, often-chorused tone.

EXERCISE II

Strum this so that the top E string is kept ringing. The final B7sus4 chord can be fretted by a conventional barre, with your index finger raised from the top E and B strings.

Emaj7	Cmaj7	Bm	Fmaj7	Emaj7	Cmaj7	Am9	B7sus4
0	0	0	0	0	0	0	0
9	8	0	10	0	8	0	0
8	9	7	9	7	9	5	8
9	9	9	10	9	9	7	7
7		9	8	9		7	9
	8	7		7	8	5	7

Emaj7	Cmaj7	Bm	Fmaj7	Emaj7	Cmaj7	Am9	B7sus4
0	0	0	0	0	0	0	0
9	8	0	10	0	8	0	0
8	9	7	9	7	9	5	8
9	9	9	10	9	9	7	7
7		9	8	9		7	9
	8	7		7	8	5	7

Kurt Cobain–Style Grunge

In 1992, the Seattle-based subculture of grunge was thrust to international musical prominence with the commercial success of Nirvana's breakthrough album *Nevermind*. Its angst-ridden songs of shattered hopes and lives that fall short of an apple-pie ideal resonated with young people everywhere.

Many of Nirvana's songs simmer with quiet expressiveness in the verses before exploding into a chorus like a teenage temper tantrum. In this, Cobain was influenced by 1980s indie bands such as Sonic Youth and The Pixies.

It's down to your drummer to create much of this effect, but it's also achieved by the contrast between picked, arpeggiated riffing (often palm-muted with your picking hand) alternated with strummed chord passages. This is especially true of the deep, dark selection of tunings that Cobain used, borrowed from Black Sabbath's Tony Iommi: whole tone (bottom D, G, C, F, A, top D); drop D (see pages 132 and 133); and drop C# (C#, G#, C#, F#, A#, D#), Cobain's invention (mixing the voicings of drop-D tuning with Hendrix's habit of tuning down a half-step

for extra impact) and one he used from the start of his recording career until its premature end in 1994.

Exercise I features an arpeggiated Nirvana-style intro or verse riff in E minor, mixing a diad power chord with a fifth in the bass (a grunge staple) and arpeggios. It's given in tuning that's dropped down a whole tone (see page 148).

Exercise II is a more chordal riff in F. Experiment with degrees of damping using your picking-hand palm across the bridge. The crosses in the tab represent muted chords—a technique that Hendrix used to double snare-drum beats. They are percussive and driving, while adding nothing to the harmony—which can be useful at times. Play them by releasing your fretting-hand fingers from the frets without removing them from the strings, while maintaining your picking-hand technique.

 **TRACK 93**

EXERCISE I

Dropping your tuning by a whole tone will make this simple E-to-D riff sound full of portent.

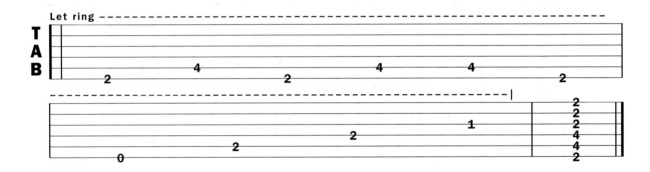

Kurt Cobain

Heavily influenced by punk and a staunch advocate of alternative rock, Kurt Cobain had a huge influence on alt rock and is remembered as one of the most iconic musicians in the genre.

SETTING THE TONE

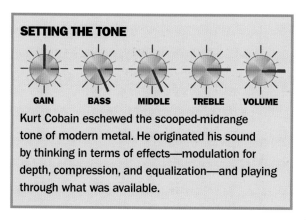

GAIN	BASS	MIDDLE	TREBLE	VOLUME

Kurt Cobain eschewed the scooped-midrange tone of modern metal. He originated his sound by thinking in terms of effects—modulation for depth, compression, and equalization—and playing through what was available.

TRACK 94

EXERCISE II

A harmonically ambiguous riff owing to power-chord voicings (with no third) and the introduction of a non-diatonic ♭VI chord (D♭5).

```
T
A
B
        3        3     x     x     x        3     3     3
        3        3     x     x     x        3     3     3
        1        1     x     x     x        1     1     1


        6        6     x     x     x     5     5     5
        6        6     x     x     x     5     5     5        3
        4        4     x     x     x     3     3     3        3
                                                              1
```

"I was looking for something a lot heavier, yet melodic at the same time. Something different from heavy metal, a different attitude."

Kurt Cobain (Nirvana)

Rage Against the Machine–
Style Riffs

During their heyday in the 1990s, rap-rock acts fused metal guitar styles and US hardcore punk beats with hip-hop influences such as Africa Bambaataa and Public Enemy. At that time, Rage Against the Machine was just one act in a firmament featuring Suicidal Tendencies, among others. Today, they're preeminent, demonstrating musical and political commitment and staying power.

RATM achieve part of their dynamism with time-signature changes that are complex but nonetheless couldn't sound less like prog rock. Tom Morello creates guitar parts brimming with sheer attitude, creating volleys of heavy rock-rap riffs powerful enough to riot to.

Morello uses heavily effected guitar sounds, which include copious flanging and the use of a pitch-shifter pedal, which he couples with his tone controls to simulate the sounds of a hip-hop DJ's scratching technique. Nevertheless, his licks are blues-based, as is his use of drop-D tuning for strong fifth power chords (see pages 130 and 131). Rhythmically, a strong, funky strumming-hand technique is heard in songs like "Testify" and "Killing in the Name." Exercises I and II feature single-note and double-stop riffs that should be played with distortion,

and accurate right- and left-hand damping for a staccato (low-value notes, with silences in between) rather than a legato feel. Tom Morello even uses a "kill" switch, which mutes his guitar's signal, for this purpose.

> ❝Music is not some stuffy college lecture. On a good day, Rage Against the Machine is not able to just rock you like a hurricane, but also to fuel the engine with indignation and the band's activist convictions.❞
>
> *Tom Morello* (Rage Against the Machine)

TRACK 95

EXERCISE I

A drop-D tuned riff that alternates palm-muted single-note runs with power chords.

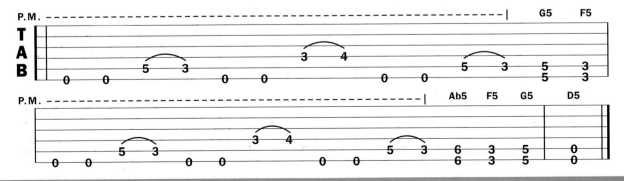

WAH-WAH SOUNDS

Before Tom Morello's use of a vibrato pedal, there was wah, pioneered by Hendrix as the most expressive effect around. A classic sound that's frequently overused, you can use it judiciously in these four ways:

Pickup-selector wah effect: Turn down the tone on your neck pickup and turn it up on your bridge pickup—toggle your selector switch in time to the music for wah without a pedal.

Wailing, blues-style: Hendrix, Hammett, or Robin Trower—a classic, broad, "Cry Baby"-style sweep that requires a slower, single treadle action on your pedal across sustained lead lines, either from open to closed or vice versa. Like a brass player's mute, this effect can really talk.

Funk rhythm-style: Curtis Mayfield, The Stone Roses, The Red Hot Chili Peppers—similar to

a "touch-wah" (one where the sweep is controlled by your playing), the pedal is rocked in time with your rhythm part and a concise sweep repeated in time with the chord progression or riff.

Tone control: Slash, Michael Schenker—keeping the pedal cocked in the middle of its travel while you play will add a classic "honking" or "quacking" tone to your arsenal.

With some wahs you can tweak the overall tonal range in advance to avoid it being too muted in its closed position.

You may wish to invest in a wah with a "true bypass" switch, as wahs can color the tone of your signal when you are not using them, muting some of the higher frequencies of otherwise bright single-coil sounds.

 TRACK 96

EXERCISE II

A simple power-chord riff in A, with single-note pentatonic runs, which derives its effectiveness from speed and accuracy.

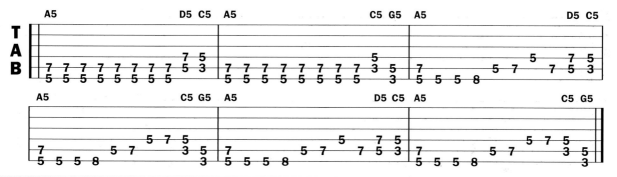

Radiohead-Style
Tricks and Textures

Radiohead released their first single, "Creep," in 1992, an imaginative serving of personal insecurity that owed its quiet verses and loud choruses to grunge, and something of its chord progression to 1960s British band The Hollies. However, it's their 1994 album *The Bends* and *OK Computer* (1995) that most show off the skills and sounds that have since proved hugely influential and which led to worldwide commercial success beyond that of any of their catchier "Britpop" peers.

With a studious image that belies the visceral rock impact of their arrangements, guitarists Jonny Greenwood and Ed O'Brien focus on textures and sound for its own sake as much as they do on complex composition—it's not surprising they would later develop an interest in electronic music. Their extensive—but never gratuitous—deployment of effects is an object lesson in how to use them without letting them use you. Tremolo and delay, for example, are set to "tap tempo;" i.e., in time with the music, and modulation effects such as flanging are used to add color to plangent, *largo* (slow) passages rather than being allowed to obscure complex harmonic ones.

One such textural technique is explored in Exercise I. Playing octaves as a lead part is not new (and was a Hendrix favorite), but coupling them with fast, tremolo picking creates a unique, driving sound. Open strings should be damped to avoid them ringing out of key, especially the string between your two fretted ones, in this case D. At slower tempos, octaves coupled with "violining" (see box) can be very expansive.

Exercise II features a harmonized rhythm riff in E major. This means that the melody has been incorporated into it by virtue of the color notes—fourths and elevenths (see pages 156 and 157)—forming a cadence in themselves. The A is a first inversion, with a C# in the bass, from which the "sus4" is easily hammered on.

 **TRACK 97**

EXERCISE I

Damp the D string with the side of the tip of your index finger to play this dramatic, ascending octave run cleanly.

```
        C    V    ◻    V    ◻    V    ◻        Eb   V    ◻    V    ◻    V    ◻    V
T ||----9----9----9----9----9----9---11--||--12---12---12---12---12---12---12---12--
A ||----7----7----7----7----7----7----9--||--10---10---10---10---10---10---10---10--
B ||------------------------------------||----------------------------------------

     Ab                                        G                              C
  ||--13---13---13---13---13---13---15--||--16---16---16---16---16---16---16--|--17--||
  ||--11---11---11---11---11---11---13--||--14---14---14---14---14---14---14--|--15--||
  ||------------------------------------||-----------------------------------|------||
```

Jonny Greenwood
Famously injured—he had to wear a brace on his arm—by his own "abusive" guitar style, Jonny Greenwood's range of unusual musical textures helped define Radiohead's distinctive sound—particularly his use of distortion and bursts of muted guitar on "Creep"—and pushed their musical boundaries in decidedly non-rock directions.

VIOLINING

"Violining"—an "onboard" guitar effect that Radiohead and many others use—is easiest on a Strat-type guitar but possible on most. Turn your guitar's volume down, fret a note, and be ready to turn the volume up again by running the outside of your fourth finger against the knob. The late Roy Buchanan was a master of this technique.

 TRACK 98

EXERCISE II

Try to achieve "pinch harmonics" by picking the B string over the 17th fret (changing to the 18th in bar 6), brushing the string with the side of your thumb as you do so.

Original Alternative Rock Tune

The following tracks consist of a lead riff and verse-chord progression with the feel of a 1990s "Britpop"-era single: full diatonic barre chord voicings give a strong sense of tonality; the evocative, clean lead licks (and quarter-tone bends) could be from a 1960s beat group, while the rhythm part owes a debt to melodic new wave bands such as The Only Ones. It follows a straightforward E–B–D–A–E–B–A–B (ending on the dominant to begin the cycle again), while the D adds harmonic color thanks to an added fourth at the top of the chord and a third in the bass (see page 159).

The chorus is more expansive, signalled by an E7#9, and rocking, in a 1990s American alt rock style, with A7 and B7 suspended fourths, with a repeating, hypnotic arpeggiated lead line. Passages of uneven lengths, Foo Fighters–style, resolve naturalistically to the dominant (B), ready for a return to the verse.

Meanwhile, the solo uses the minor pentatonic and minor blues scales over a driving break that goes to the minor third—C#min (which has already appeared at the end of the chorus) /A/Ab. Aspects such as the

irregular chorus and its added four-bar ending lick, over a I–♭III–IV–V progression, represent the alternative rocker's desire to cherry-pick the best classic-rock techniques and express them concisely, but to keep pushing at the confines of the genre and to throw in a few surprises that, if they sound right, can't be wrong!

TRACK 99

The Only Ones
Peter Perrett was the lead singer for The Only Ones. This British rock 'n' roll band started in the late 1970s and was associated with punk rock, yet broadened into areas that fell musically between punk, power pop, and hard rock—with some noticeable influences from psychedelia. Their biggest hit, "Another Girl, Another Planet," was a huge UK hit, and their influence on the indie rock and alternative rock scenes has been apparent ever since in bands such as The Replacements, Blur, Nirvana, and, more recently, The Libertines.

VERSE

CHORUS

BREAK

Chord
Directory

These chord boxes cover some of the equivalent chord types for keys other than those given on pages 24 and 25, together with giving some key-specific examples of the movable shapes featured on pages 30 and 31. It also includes the chord shapes that appear in specific exercises throughout the book. You'll see that some of these, though given in specific keys, are useful movable chord shapes too.

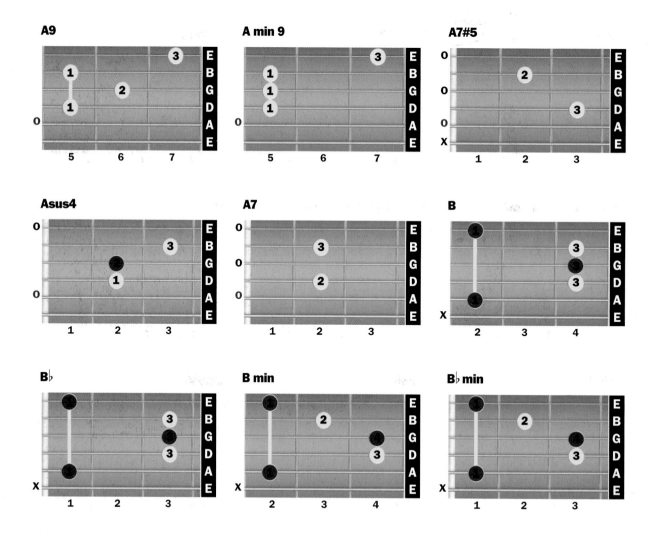

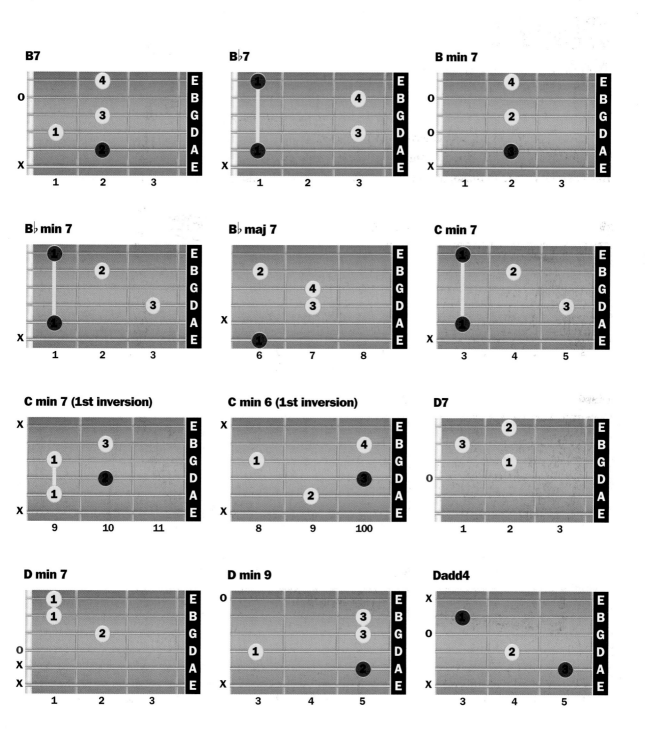

B7

B♭7

B min 7

B♭ min 7

B♭ maj 7

C min 7

C min 7 (1st inversion)

C min 6 (1st inversion)

D7

D min 7

D min 9

Dadd4

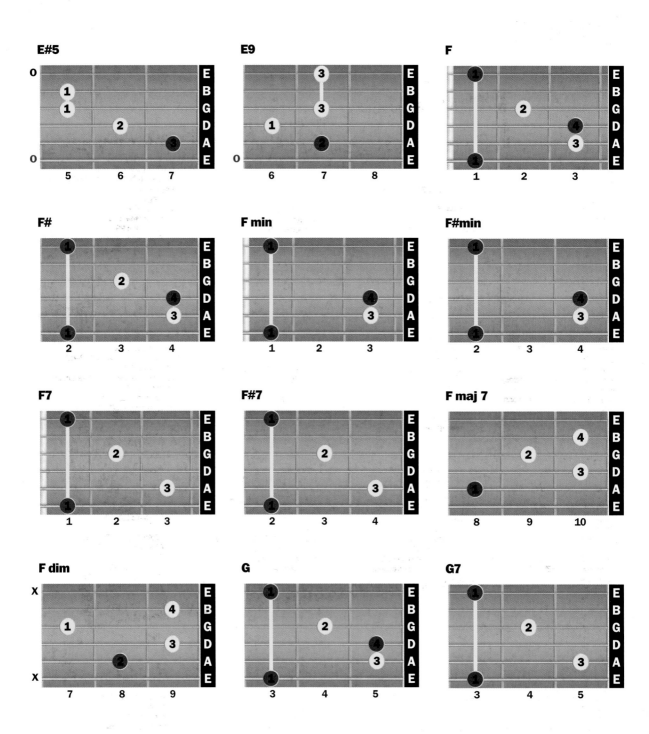

Index

Acknowledgments

Marshall Editions would like to thank the following for their kind permission to reproduce their images.

Key: t = top   b = bottom

Pages: 2–3 ® Gibson Flying V; 4–5 Alamy/Simon Clay; 6–7 Shutterstock; 8–9 Getty Images/Wire Image/Marty Temme; 10–11 Shutterstock/Mny-Jhee/Fender Telecaster® ; Shutterstock/M E Mulder/Fender Stratocaster ® ; Getty Images/Redferns/ Geoff Dann/Gretsch Nashville ® ; Alamy/Simon Clay Rickenbecker. ® Gibson Flying V; 13 Shutterstock/Ilker Canikligil; 14 Getty Images/Redferns/Mick Hutson; 15t Corbis/Icon SMI/Paul Herbert; 15b Rex Features/ITV Archive; 19 courtesy of Marshall Amplification plc; 20–21 Shutterstock; 26–27 Marshall Editions; 29 Rex Features/Debra L Rothenberg; 32 Rex Features/Marc Sharrat; 35 Rex Features/Most Wanted; 37 Getty Images/Stringer/Paul Kane; 38–39 Shutterstock; 41Rex Features/ILPO/MUSTO; 43 Getty Images/Michael Ochs Archives/Jim Steinfeldt; 45 Getty Images/Wire Image/ Marty Temme; 47 Getty Images/Redferns/ Brigitte Engl; 49 Rex Features/Andre Csillag; 51 Rex Features; 52–53 Shutterstock; 59 Getty Images/Redferns/David Redfern; 61 Corbis/Christopher Felver; 65 Getty Images/Ed Rode; 67 Getty Images/Michael Ochs Archive/Larry Hulst; 70 Getty Images/Redferns/Joe Satriani; 72–73 Getty Images/Stringer/Roger Kisby; 79 Getty Images/WireImage/Kevin Mazur; 81 Rex Features/Canadian Press; 83 Getty Images/Redferns/David Redfern; 90–91 Getty Images/ Redferns /Geoff Dann; 92 Rex Features; 95 Getty Images/Stringer/Michael Ochs Archive; 97 Rex Features/George Konig; 101 Getty Images/Redferns/Petra Niemeier; 103 Getty Images/Stringer/Michael Ochs Archive; 104 Getty Images/Stringer/ Michael Ochs Archive; 108–109 Shutterstock; 110 Getty Images/Redferns/Fin Costello; 112 Getty Images/Redferns/Keith Bernstein; 114 Getty Images/Redferns/Dick Barnatt; 118 Rex Features/ Ian Dickson; 122 Getty Images/Kevin Winter; 126–127 courtesy of Fender Musical Instruments Corporation, Arizona; 131 Getty Images/Scott Legato/Film Magic; 133 Getty Images/WireImage/Brian Killian; 135 Getty Images/Redferns/George De Sota; 136 Corbis/Neal Preston; 141 Getty Images/Tim Mosenfelder; 143 Getty Images/ Noel Vasquez; 145 Rex Features/Ville Myllynen; 147 Getty Images/Redferns/Mick Hutson; 148 Rex Features/Brian Rasic; 154–155 Fender; 157 Rex Features/Dezo Hoffman; 159 Getty Images/Hulton Archive; 161 Rex Features/ Andre Csillag; 163 Getty Images/Redferns/Ian Dickson; 165 Rex Features; 166 Getty Images/Claire R Greenway; 170–171 Shutterstock/Scoutingstock; 172 Getty Images/Redferns/Richard E. Aaron; 175 Getty Images/Redferns/Frank Micelotta; 177 Getty Images/Redferns/Gary Wolstenholme; 179 Getty Images/Film Magic/Jeff Kravitz; 183 Getty Images/Redferns/Paul Bergen; 184 Getty Images/Redferns/C Brandon.

FENDER® , TELECASTER® , and the distinctive headstock design of those guitars are trademarks owned by Fender Musical Instruments Corporation. All rights reserved. JACKSON® , is a trademark owned by Jackson/Charvel Maufacturing, Inc. All rights reserved. Gretsch® is a trademark of Fred W Gretsch Enterprises, Ltd and is used herein with express written permission.